JUSTICE, JUSTICE SHALL YOU PURSUE:
A HISTORY OF NEW JEWISH AGENDA
BY
EZRA BERKLEY NEPON

---

*for Jake! ♡
love to you &
thrilled to be in
community w/ you
politically & neighborly
♡ Ezra Berkley
Nepon*

Justice, Justice, Shall You Pursue: A History of New Jewish Agenda
by Ezra Berkley Nepon

2012 Thread Makes Blanket Press/ Ezra Berkley Nepon

ISBN 0-9727072-3-9

Thread Makes Blanket is a small press that embarks on collaborations with artists and authors to produce books of substance and beauty. With a wealth of collective knowledge and effort supporting the press, Thread Makes Blanket comes out of community.

Thread Makes Blanket Press
4953 Catharine St
Philadelphia, PA 19143
www.threadmakesblanket.com

Printed at:
1984 Printing
674-B 23rd Street
Oakland, CA 94612
www.1984printing.com

CONTENTS

PREFACE

his book is a labor of love, a do-it-yourself publication, a people's history of Jewish progressive and radical activism throughout the 1980s. This is a story about thousands of Jewish activists working for liberation and social transformation while wrestling with anti-Semitism, and challenging internal community issues including sexism, homophobia, racism, and classism. And this is a story about thousands of Jewish-Americans working in solidarity with liberation struggles of African-Americans, Arab-Americans, Central Americans, Palestinians, and other communities under attack during a decade defined by the brutal policies of the Reagan Administration. The story of New Jewish Agenda (NJA) has a lot to teach Jewish activists of younger generations and anyone who thinks curiously, critically, or creatively about how social movements build, evolve, and bring about transformations.

I came to this research as a next-generation Jewish activist, uncovering the not-so-distant history that informed my own political and personal life. I was born in 1978, two years before New Jewish Agenda's founding conference. I was raised in Reform Judaism, a fifth-generation descendant of one of the first Reform rabbis in the US. I grew up in rural New Jersey, where my parents co-founded a small congregation. There, my father served as the lay rabbi and I attended Torah study sessions in my family's living room. At age ten, my family moved to Allentown, PA and joined a more established Jewish community where I attended Sunday School, Hebrew School, and Confirmation Class. In high school I was president of my local youth group, and attended national NFTY (Reform youth group) conferences and leadership development events.

And yet, while my sense of justice, my ethics, and my yearning for a better world were so deeply tied to Jewish cultural and spiritual identity, I was aware of differences that left me questioning how to be my full self in Jewish community. Most glaringly, I never felt connected to Israel as a place representing safety and justice in the ways

I heard family and community members refer to it. The first Palestinian intifada broke out around the time I started Sunday School, and I remember being taught that Israel was the one thing keeping us safe. I looked at a map of tiny Israel and sensed that there was no way all the Jews could fit into those borders. I remember attending pro-Israel rallies at youth group events, and feeling uncomfortably aware of the group-think we were encouraged to perform, frustrated with the simplicity of the nationalist messages. I also remember my fear the first time I heard progressive activists criticizing Israel, and how terrified I felt the first time I attended a rally in solidarity with Palestinians. I saw my Jewish community turning our real fears and grief into defensive anger and aggression, and I knew I had to seek out a different path.

That path led me to New Jewish Agenda. In 2003, I was reading all the Jewish feminist writing I could get my hands on, and references to NJA kept showing up all over back issues of *Bridges* Journal and books by inspiring activists like Melanie Kaye/Kantrowitz, Irena Klepfisz, and Elly Bulkin. I was curious about this organization that so many profound movement builders, writers, and thinkers had been part of. I went looking for a book or good long article to learn more. You can usually find multiple Jewish opinions about everything under the sun, so I assumed that I'd be able to savor a wealth of resources. I found almost nothing, and my curiosity was further sparked by the strange lack of record.

I searched for the stories of New Jewish Agenda over the course of three years: poring over original sources at the Tamiment radical history archives at NYU's Bobst Library, interviewing seven former members, reading every relevant book I could get my hands on, and asking every Jewish activist I met what they remembered about NJA. I only met one other person under thirty who had heard of NJA. When I talked to my peers about my research, the responses were dramatic. Like me, they were hungry for these stories.

My passion for documenting NJA's story comes from a strong desire for a community like the one they created. Digging through archive boxes, interviewing members, and sharing what I learned makes me feel part of something exciting that I was too young to join in the 1980s. I researched NJA for the same reasons many became members: to feel less isolated as a Jewish progressive or radical, to connect with more diverse communities of activists, to gain insight into strategies for activism infused with cultural and spiritual meaning, to feel part of a powerful legacy, to imagine a future with liberatory possibility.

In 2006, I put much of my research online as a website, including links to many original documents. And now, finally, I'm thrilled to publish this book - an expanded reporting and analysis of New Jewish Agenda's history that can be passed from hand to hand. It has been exciting to prepare this text in the context of the newly-emerging Occupy Movement and especially Occupy Judaism, whose slogan "Bringing the Jews to Occupy Wall Street. Bringing Occupy Wall Street to the Jews" is reminiscent of NJA's mission. Occupy Judaism's 2011 emergence with Occupy Yom Kippur led to Occupy Sukkot, Occupy Shabbat, and an evolving new national and local opportunity to offer -as NJA put it - "a Jewish voice among progressives and a progressive voice among Jews." Occupy Judaism's use of Jewish cultural and religious tropes, open letters from rabbis and other community leaders, and willingness to stand up to right-wing Jewish fearmongering are further evidence of both NJA's historical influence and the engaged participation of movement elders who used those same strategies in NJA. Occupy Judaism is a reminder that New Jewish Agenda wasn't the first example of widespread Jewish progressive and radical organizing, by far, and it certainly won't be the last. This snapshot of a decade of organizing, wrestling, and sometimes winning Jewish struggles for justice is offered as a tool that can help us move forward grounded in the roots of our work today, building on lessons learned, reaching for ever more distant goals.

In gerangl/Yours in that struggle,

Ezra Berkley Nepon

THANK-YOU:
Marissa Johnson-Valenzuela and Eric Kane of Thread Makes Blanket; Daniel Rosza Lang/Levitsky, Rachel Mattson, and Abigail Miller for political and culture-making partnership on this and many other projects; Simone Zelitch for excellent feedback; Jenny Berkley for editing support and insights; publishing wisdom from Cleo Woeffle-Erskine; and creative inspiration from justseeds.org's Celebrate People's History poster series. Thank you to each of the supporters who helped us raise the funds to publish this book by pre-ordering and donating. Especially my deepest thanks to those I interviewed for generously sharing their stories, and to those whose feminist, queer, radical Jewish writing inspired me to go looking for this story in the first place.

A HISTORY OF NEW JEWISH AGENDA

New Jewish Agenda (NJA, or often abbreviated as "Agenda") was a national membership organization active between 1980 and 1992 with the slogan "a Jewish voice among progressives and a progressive voice among Jews."[1] NJA practiced participatory grassroots democracy with five-thousand members in over forty-five local chapters, and organized for justice through National Task Forces on Middle East Peace, Worldwide Nuclear Disarmament, Economic and Social Justice, Central American Solidarity, and Jewish Feminism. NJA took radical stances on the rights of Palestinians and Queer Jews, and organized a Jewish presence in movements throughout the 1980s. Jewish activists from a wide range of religious and secular communities coalesced in NJA, building power and analysis that continue to illuminate progressive Jewish activism.

Ronald Reagan was elected the 40th U.S. President, unseating incumbent Democrat Jimmy Carter, on November 4, 1980 - two months before the NJA Founding Convention. NJA emerged as a center for Jewish Left organizing at a time of profound rightward shift in the U.S. The Reagan agenda would become known for brutally cutting resources for the U.S.'s poor and low-income, breaking unions, and generally centralizing wealth in what we now call "the 1%"; for supporting military terror in Central America, the Middle East, Argentina, Grenada, and around the globe; for the Iran-Contra scandal and the Savings & Loans crisis; for an obsessive battle against Communism; and for staying silent as the AIDS pandemic swept the nation and the world.

NJA faced a major task in organizing a grassroots movement, but they were not inventing the wheel – the founders came from diverse movements and political cultures that offered wisdom and strength for the journey.

---

1   I found this slogan in NJA's official literature only once – on a 1987 organizational brochure – but this phrase was consistently used by my interviewees to describe the organization.

Seeking Alternatives:
The Legacy of Breira and a Call for a New Jewish Agenda

The first seeds of New Jewish Agenda came during the final board meeting of a group called *Breira: A Project of Concern in Diaspora-Israel Relations*. The name, Hebrew for "Alternative," was a response to the common phrase "*Ain breira*" or "There is no alternative" an Israeli Labor Party slogan used to justify military aggression much in the way "National Security" is used in today's American political rhetoric. In *Torn at the Roots*, Michael Staub quotes national chairperson Rabbi Arnold Jacob Wolf about the mission of Breira:

> The name betokened our desire for an alternative (*breira* in Hebrew) to the intransigence of both the Palestinian Liberation Organization (PLO) and the several governments of Israel. We proposed what has come to be known as the two-state solution, now more than ever the chief possibility for a peaceful, long-term resolution of the Middle East conflict.[2]

Breira was founded just a few months before Israel's 1973 Yom Kippur War (also known as the Ramadan War), which heralded an unprecedented level of financial and other support from American Jews to Israel. While Breira's work to encourage dialogue and recognition of the rights of Palestinians was at first met with relatively positive reviews from Jewish press and organizations, the group's position grew increasingly marginalized, and they were eventually destroyed by a brutal smear campaign.

Breira advocated within the American Jewish community for a two-state solution, and offered amplification to the growing Israeli community that shared their politics. Breira challenged mainstream Jewish organizations for censoring critiques of Israeli policies, and urged members to withhold financial support in protest. Breira's organizing was threatening to right-wing Jewish organizations, especially those connected to Jewish settlements in the Palestinian territories, and the organization was aggressively taken down within five embattled years.

---

2   Michael E. Staub. *Torn at the Roots: the Crisis of Jewish Liberalism in Postwar America.* (New York: Columbia University Press, 2002), 280-308.

Their most prominent detractor was Americans for a Safe Israel
(AFSI).

In 1977, AFSI's Rael Jean Isaac wrote a thirty-page pamphlet called
"Breira: Counsel for Judaism," sharply critiquing Breira for speaking
out about Israel as American Jews. The mainstream Jewish community
received Isaac's rejection of Breira as a neutral report, but in fact Isaac
had not disclosed that she was an advisory board member of an Israeli
settlement movement, *Gush Emunim*, that Breira had been challenging.
Isaac's pamphlet accused Breira of allegiance with the Palestinian Liberation Organization (PLO), and painted a picture of a dangerous organization bent on the destruction of Israel. At the time, any recognition of Palestinian nationalism was seen as treasonous betrayal within
the Jewish community - and any visibility of a diversity of Jewish
opinions was seen in mainstream circles as airing of dirty laundry that
threatened to seriously hurt Israel's safety. Isaac also used a redbaiting[3]
strategy: a good two thirds of the pamphlet decries Breira's affiliation with the radical New Left[4] by targeting member Arthur Waskow,
a well-known Jewish activist involved in many progressive protests
including the 1968 Chicago DNC, and author of the first *Freedom Seder*
which brought together Jewish and Black activists on the first anniversary of the assassination of Rev. Martin Luther King, Jr.[5]

Isaac's smear campaign did irreparable damage. Opponents in the
mainstream Jewish community labeled Breira a PLO front group, Jewish organizations fired many of those affiliated with Breira, and other
Jewish groups picketed Breira gatherings with signs such as "Death to
Breira" and "Breira Means Suicide." The group was discredited and
politically paralyzed within the Jewish community.

Coming out of the traumatizing end of Breira, many believed that the
organization had been especially vulnerable because it was a single-
issue group, and because it had a large steering committee of Jewish
community leaders but had never built a truly grassroots movement.

---

3 Redbaiting is the act of smearing/discrediting someone by accusing them of affiliation with
Leftist causes including Communism, Socialism, etc.
4 New Left was a term associated with hippie and college campus activism in the 1960's and
70's
5 Rael Jean Isaac. *Breira: Counsel for Judaism*. (New York: Americans for a Safe Israel, 1977).

NJA founder Rabbi Gerry Serotta recalls that at the end of Breira's organizational life, he turned to John Ruskay (one of Breira's founders and Serotta's roommate at the time) and asked, "What are we going to do next? Who's going to start a successor organization?" Ruskay told Serotta, "You do it!"

Rabbi Serotta and his local Breira chapter (Rutgers, NJ) wrote a "New Jewish Manifesto," a multi-issue progressive Jewish statement that could be used as an outreach and organizing tool. Next, in December 1978, Serotta met with Jewish campus organization directors at the national Hillel conference. Many in that group shared Serotta's feelings of alienation within the mainstream Jewish community, and expressed a need for a forum to organize as progressive Jews. Coming out of the Hillel meeting, there were two competing strategies: a new organization or a move to advocate for a broader agenda within existing groups. To explore the latter possibility, Serotta and Brandeis Hillel Director Al Axelrad went to a board meeting of Americans for Progressive Israel (API), a socialist-Zionist group, to encourage a shift to "Americans for Progressive *Klal* Israel."[6] API expressed some interest, but this strategy did not generate the same energy as visions of a new organization. Most of the Hillel community wanted to work within an organization that would be broadly focused (beyond Israel) from the beginning.

In May 1979, following the circulation of a "Call for a 1980 Congress of Progressive Jews," Serotta invited two hundred Jewish Left leaders to gather in New York.[7] Fifty arrived to discuss and strategize organizational options for progressive Jews. By Serotta's memory, half of the attendees were women and 10-20% were Jewish professionals such as rabbis and educators. That meeting created the Organizing Committee for a New Jewish Agenda (OCNJA), a name suggested by Jewish Left scholar-activist Jack Jacobs, and set the goal of holding a national Jewish conference to establish a "new Jewish agenda."

It was not immediately clear to the early organizers that this national conference would lead to creation of a national organization. Reena Bernards, national director of NJA between 1981-1986, suggested that the grassroots desire for a membership organization combined with

---

6   Klal Israel means "all the people Israel", the global Jewish community rather than the nation.
7   Included in this volume, see Appendix I

the hesitancy of the conference organizers to commit to that goal may have contributed to insecurities people brought to the conference, and resulting power struggles over the platform.

Multiple Agendas:
Progressive Jews and Jewish Progressives

In "Jewish Renewal," an article published in the magazine *Genesis 2* shortly before the 1980 founding conference, Gerry Serotta reflected on the reality that approximately 50% of American Jews were unaffiliated with any organization, and spoke to NJA's desire to create a "home for progressive Jews.[8]" But who were those Jews? Christie Balka, former national co-chair of NJA, recalls that "there were a few different tropes in Agenda." First, there were those Jews with progressive politics, who were not engaged in Jewish community. Of this constituency, Serotta said "one of our definite goals [was] to involve the unaffiliated, disaffiliated, and especially those alienated from the politics of the American Jewish community - those who feel that it has turned so rightward and inward that they can no longer feel comfortable in the community." Balka says that this included a number of ex-Students for a Democratic Society (SDS) members who had not previously been "Jewishly" identified but for whom this was the next movement they could connect with since SDS's disintegration. Balka identifies herself as of this first trope. She was raised in a secular household, and graduated from the Quaker school system in Philadelphia. In NJA, Balka found a way to connect with her Jewishness while living in Ann Arbor, MI and working in a Quaker peace organization. She went on to become National Co-Chair of the organization, co-wrote a book about being Jewish and Gay, and later helped found a progressive synagogue in Philadelphia.

The second type of person attracted to NJA was deeply involved in Jewish communities and looking for a way to connect with progressive politics from a Jewish position. Balka remembers many NJA members who had attended leadership training programs, either through Reform or Conservative congregational youth groups or Socialist-Zionist youth programs like Habonim. These young people had continued on

---

8   Donny Perlstein and Rabbi Gerry Serotta. "Jewish Renewal: The birth of an organization whose time has come." *Genesis 2* Sep. - Oct. 1980.

to college and were looking for a way to plug in. Serotta also talked about "dissident establishmentarians," rabbis and other members of mainstream Jewish organizations who were fed up with working for slow institutional changes.

Looking back, Serotta remembers the two critical letters he received in response to the initial invitation to the first OCNJA meeting as a telling sign of things to come. Arthur Waskow wrote that NJA would be irrelevant if it became just another secular Jewish organization critical of the Jewish community. To succeed it would have to be spiritually rooted. Waskow came to the meeting anyway, and presented a number of workshops at the Founding Conference. Eli Schaap, a recent immigrant from Holland who had been an active Jewish socialist there, said it wouldn't work because there was no thriving American Left to be part of. Still, Schaap came to the first meeting as well, and he became the treasurer of OCNJA and chairperson of the Conference Committee. Looking back, Serotta thinks that they were both correct. He believes that many of the leaders of NJA lacked connection to Jewish culture, which often made NJA weak in terms of "Jewishness." Simultaneously, the weakness of the American Left in terms of divisive infighting, lack of strategy, and process over politics created a situation where NJA remained marginal in both the Jewish and general communities. In another way, Waskow and Schaap's critiques predicted a positive trend in the organization. While New Jewish Agenda took on the mission of serving as "A Progressive Voice in the Jewish Community and a Jewish Voice Among Progressives," there were always deep tensions between those constituents who thought NJA wasn't doing enough in the Jewish community or in the secular progressive movement. Nevertheless, both communities showed up and stayed invested.

Founding Convention, Christmas 1980

By the time of the conference, there were 2,000 people on the OCNJA mailing list. In San Francisco, Ann Arbor, Detroit, and Boston, local groups had already formed in response to OCNJA's initial national organizing efforts. OCNJA members mobilized attendees by attending the Havurah conference[9], and the Conference on Al-

---

9   The National Havurah Committee, which produces this annual conference, is a network of diverse individuals and communities dedicated to Jewish living and learning, community building,

ternatives in Jewish Education (CAJE), and networking with existing radical Jewish collectives like Chutzpah in Chicago, Boston Committee to Challenge Anti-Semitism, Project on New Jewish Alternatives in Madison, and Kadima in Seattle.

Over 700 people attended NJA's founding conference at the 4H-Conference Center in Washington, D.C. on December 25, 1980, and over 300 more were turned away for lack of space. The choice of date was not random, as Christmas is usually a day when American Jews face alienation in our officially secular, but Christian-dominated, national culture. The conference featured a few different tracks: educational sessions focused on Jewish progressive approaches to historical and modern political and social issues; creation of a "conference community" through religious and cultural events, caucuses, and get-to-know-you exercises; and, not least important, the work of creating a national organization through adoption of a Conference Unity statement, By-Laws, and Task Forces.

A sampling of workshop presenters can offer a glimpse into the rich diversity of voices that were gathered for the conference: NYC City Council Member Ruth Messinger, who went on to direct American Jewish World Services; Michael Lerner, who went on to found *Tikkun Magazine* and the Tikkun Network, identified as a spiritual leader, director of the Institute for Labor and Mental Health, and a defendant in the Seattle 8 Conspiracy Trial; Aviva Cantor, editor of *Lilith Magazine* and founding member of the Jewish Liberation Project; Yiddishist Henry Sapoznik; Allen Solomonow of the Middle East Peace Project; Michael Strassfeld, co-editor of *The Jewish Catalogues*; Rhonda Weiss, attorney for the U.S. Dept. of Education; Sam Norich, Vice-President of the World Jewish Congress. Workshop topics ranged from "Jews, Agriculture, and Rural America" to "Prayerbook in One Hand, Newspaper in the Other" to "The Rise of the New Right."[10]

In a *New Jewish Times* article, attendee Jonathan Mark offered an entertaining report on the founding conference's decision-making process. Mark notes that on the second day of the conference, attendees

and *tikkun olam* (repairing the world). NHC is an organization that provides resources and networks to grassroots Jewish communities, and does not have any formal category of congregational affiliation.

10   New Jewish Agenda, "Conference For A New Jewish Agenda for the 1980's" (Booklet, Washington DC, 1980)

voted to formulate not only a broad unity statement, but also specific amendments on controversial issues including the Middle East.
Though work to create the Unity Statement had been going on for
over six months leading up to the conference, there would only be two
days for writing, debating, and voting on the amendments.

An all-group Havdalah (ending Sabbath) service at nine o'clock on
Saturday night brought the attendees together in a moment of singing
and holding hands. Then the lights came on and it was "time for battle
over agenda by-laws." Word-by-word debate over the by-law pro-
posal went on for hours, as Mark explained "the procedure is almost
paralyzed from the start by games of parliamentary jabberwocky and
Talmudical fishing expeditions in which trivial 'points of procedure,'
'points of information,' and 'points of clarification' produce a de facto
filibuster by delegates from across the spectrum." By half-past mid-
night only 492 of the 700 conference attendees were left, dropping
away from the tiresome process in streams and floods. Quorum called
for 328 votes.

Despite the group frustrations and tensions, a culture of Jewish humor also pervaded the proceedings. Mark remembered that at 1 a.m.
a bunch of conference participants broke the tensions with hilarious
antics:

> Merry Pranksters walk around with balloons and scaf-
> folding on their heads, mimes clown and juggle in the
> aisles, jokes are exchanged about a new organization for
> militant feminists and gays entitled 'New Jewish Gender.'
> And, to parody the dozens of single-issue caucuses, a Jew
> playing possum is carried to the center of the stage and
> announced as 'the Dead Caucus,' representing dead Jews
> everywhere and their contributions to Judaism.

The bylaws passed at 2:15 a.m., and the crowd erupted! Mark wrote,
"A wild stampede of relief and exhilaration sweeps the delegates out
of their seats and into dancing snake-lines through the aisles, swirl-
ing into circles of Israeli dancing in a demonstration that lasts over
40 minutes." Attendee Jeff Oboler is quoted in Mark's article with
the powerful reflection that this end-of-the-process celebration was
"a magnificent moment for Jews. Was there any other time in Jewish

history when Orthodox danced with Marxists, when straights danced with gays?"

At 3 a.m. a relatively moderate unity statement passed, and frustration built with the recognition that there were still a number of radical resolutions to tackle. Another much-needed moment of comic relief broke the tension. Mark described the scene: "a woman approaches the microphone and leads the delegates in The Itsy-Bitsy Spider Climbs Up the Water Spout, followed by whoops and wild applause."[11]

After two more hours of debate, the quorum was finally lost and the session recessed. Reconvened at 8:15 a.m., the last day of the conference never reached decision-making quorum. The couple of hundred attendees who showed up did pass the resolutions ("inadvertently called 'revolutions' by the caller of the roll," wrote Mark) in a straw poll, but NJA leaders were clear that Sunday's decisions would have no impact on NJA policy. These resolutions, passed by more than 70% in the straw polls, included support for a broad range of issues, from diversity and democratic decision-making within Jewish community to support for Ethiopian Jews to be taken in by Israel.

At the founding conference, a 25-member Executive Committee (EC) was elected. The EC agreed that the straw-poll resolutions should function as guides and not mandates of NJA policy, and proposed establishing task forces for each recommended area.

"Why Won't They Just Say Who They Are?"
The Controversial Impact of Re-Evaluation Counseling

NJA's founding conference brought progressive Jews of all stripes into one "big tent." It was a major accomplishment to coalesce such a large and diverse group, but clear tensions emerged early on between the divergent progressive cultures. Those conflicts would prove challenging throughout NJA's life. Rabbi Serotta remembers that among the diverse political crowd, only members of the Re-Evaluation Counseling (RC, or "co-counseling") community attended as an organized group. Re-Evaluation Counseling is an organization founded in the 1950's by

---

11   Jonathan Mark. "Toward a New Jewish Agenda: The Left's Last Chance," *New Jewish Times*, Feb/March 1981, 23-26.

Harvey Jackins, which grew to an international movement in which members train to counsel each other to heal traumatic experiences, often through sessions involving physical actions of "discharge" including laughing, crying, yawning, etc. Jackins was influenced by Marxism and the Dianetics movement, and RC places importance on political work as part of personal transformation, at times (as in the case of NJA) encouraging members to join specific organizations and take leadership.[12] It appears that Middle East peace activists with a "Breira-nik" analysis also mobilized to attend the conference as a combined force[13], however, the RC community's impact on the founding conference was more controversial among organizers and attendees.

Joined by a shared therapeutic and consciousness-raising culture, RC members were largely unaffiliated with "hard-Left"[14] movements or with organized Jewish communities. The RC group was, however, well-versed in specific detailed group-process. Other attendees reported finding their techniques frustrating, especially those who attended the convention's "Left Caucus" expecting the usual mission-driven (rather than process-driven) meeting style. Serotta remembers,

> The main problem they brought to Agenda, which was a tremendous difficulty for us in national terms, was an enormous concern for process over substance... At the founding conference some of the Leftists, serious Leftists, totally freaked out. Committed Socialists, DSA[15] types, were just aghast. They went to the Left caucus, which was mostly run by the co-counseling network and they flipped out! They said, "Where's the Left?"

---

12   This practice, and allegations of sexual abuse by Jackins against women in his therapeutic care have led many to question the RC movement's ethics and even to accuse RC of being a cult. The impact of RC on NJA was and continues to be a very controversial and emotional topic, one that came up in every interview and all of the informal conversations I had with NJA members– much more often than the infiltration of NJA by the crypto-fascist New Alliance Party. The NJA members that I interviewed are all people who were not members of RC or who have left RC, not a representative sampling. Nevertheless, I have tried to offer a relatively objective perspective.

13   Tom Smerling (a former Breira member) started The Shalom Network as Breira was ending, to continue Breira's work. The Shalom Network held a training workshop in the days before the NJA founding convention, and Shalom Network eventually merged with NJA's Middle East Task Force.

14   Sectarian membership-based movements focused on Class struggle, i.e. Marxists, Trotskyists, etc

15   Democratic Socialists of America

So we were badly hamstrung by very silly fights about process that had to do with a jargon and approach that was coming from co-counseling. None of which was wrong, it was just rigid... It led to a fact that we lost potential leadership, so it did have a long-term effect and impact on the organization and the quality of people who were willing to continue to be connected. You should see the list of people who spoke at that founding convention, and the diversity, it's an unbelievable list of people! From people who were high up in the government to just about everybody who was a Jewish progressive. But they didn't have a high tolerance for this part of our organizational culture. One could see that as an issue of elite versus grassroots, which is partly the argument that I would make to people. I mean if you want to work in the grassroots, you've got to work with *people*, but it wasn't just grassroots people. It was an organized network with a style that I thought was challenging.

This process-heavy organizational culture played out in a sort of affirmative action within leadership. RC folks insisted that a woman speak after every man, and that there be at least half women's leadership on every task force. This wasn't an altogether new idea. Even in the early '70's Breira had said in its by-laws that one-third of the national board had to be female. In fact, there were many women leaders in NJA from the earliest days, due to a strong feminist focus within OCNJA. Though few would take issue with the idea of gender equity in the leadership, the strict demands of RC-members created a challenging situation for some NJA leadership. For example, founder Gerry Serotta had to leave the steering committee early on because there were not enough women in that group. Another process-rule necessitated full regional representation in the leadership of each task force. This rule reflected a fear, held by many, that because so many Jews live in the Mid-Atlantic East Coast, concerns of Jews in other regions would be overlooked. Again, though this was an idea few would disagree with, the process-demands were laborious for the organization.

In retrospect, it may have been just these laborious policies that allowed NJA to function as a gathering place and incubator for leadership within traditionally marginalized Jewish communities: young, feminist, working class, and queer leaders emerged from NJA and went on to have powerful impacts in shaping progressive and Jewish communities. Would NJA have been just another "*macherarchy*"[16] without the demands of ultra-democracy? On the other hand, it may have contributed to NJA's marginalization as an organization attempting to bring a "new agenda" to the mainstream Jewish community.

Clare Kinberg, a national leader, Feminist Task Force staff person, and longtime editor of *Bridges Journal*, reflected on the actions that were taken to create a financially accessible organization, and the way she benefited from the "ultra-democracy" within NJA.

> One of the reasons I was able to go to that first National Council meeting was that we did something called a "travel pool," where everybody's expenses were pooled together so everybody had to pay $200, and somebody from my local chapter paid half for me to go. The idea of doing that was really important for getting a variety of people to the meeting. It was really complicated and took a ton of energy to figure out what all the expenses of the conference would be and to divide it up and make even people local to NY (when the meeting was in NY) pay $200, so that people coming from St Louis and Des Moines and San Francisco only had to pay $200. It really made a difference. [The travel pool] made it so that people could be involved. I think Reena and Jeffrey and Arthur and others became frustrated with the ultra-democracy, but it was really putting into practice an important value. It only scratched the surface of dealing with class in Agenda. There were still a lot of people who couldn't get $200 together twice a year to come to the National Council meetings. Just the idea that anybody would go to a meeting in NY two times a year was not something that was in the consciousness, because it was just out of the question for a whole lot of people who weren't middle class. I think Agenda could never really figure out how to do that. I don't know if anybody can figure out how to have a national organization that's really accessible.

---

16 *Macher* is a big shot, literally "maker" in Yiddish

One of the biggest critiques of RC's involvement in NJA was the secrecy of what was essentially an affinity group within a larger organization. Avi Rose had been an active RC member when he got involved with the NJA. He was an RC "Area Reference Person" for the Bay Area and involved in RC's work on Jewish Liberation and Gay Liberation. As a member of the first Steering Committee, Rose was part of the group tasked with addressing the controversy and confusion about RC within NJA. Rose recalled:

> Agenda came along and some RCers were naturally
> drawn to it because there were a number of progressive
> Jews in RC. But there was also some effort to get people
> involved in it to influence the direction of the organiza-
> tion, so the distressing thing was that there was an effort
> to do that and then a simultaneous denial that that's what
> people were doing. It was pretty crazy, and as a result a
> lot of the non-RCers in the organization were wondering
> "What's going on? Is there this cult or organization that's
> really trying to run the show or take over or influence us?
> Why don't they identify who they are? And why do they
> go in the corner and laugh inappropriately?" Some of the
> behavior seemed kind of bizarre to people, it was unset-
> tling for people because clearly there were a number of
> people there, but people wouldn't identify whether they
> were from RC or not. It was just really destructive, and
> there are people who left early on because of that reason.
> They just felt like maybe Agenda was some front for
> some other organization that wasn't being accountable
> and wasn't being up front, and people got the hell out of
> there.

As a member of the steering committee, Rose wrote and distributed a letter to all NJA members explaining RC and proposing that RC members should be more open about their affiliation, and should avoid using RC-jargon. Rose suggested that RC'ers should speak for themselves and not "parrot positions put forward by others," and the relationship between NJA and RC should be discussed and clarified. Also, Rose suggested that outreach be done to all NJA constituencies

to prevent one group from having disproportionate impact.[17] Rose
left RC because of controversy about that letter, as well as other concerns about RC's founder and homophobic policies.

Multi-Issue Strategy

From the earliest days of NJA, founders promoted the creation of
a solidly multi-issue platform. After Breira's fall, and cognizant of
Jewish fears about anti-Semitism on the Left, Gerry Serotta and others
worked carefully to avoid public perception as just another anti-Israel
group (that happened to be Jewish). Serotta believes that single-issue
and expert-centered organizing made Breira an easier target to destroy:

> I was on the losing faction of Breira... I was very strongly
> of the opinion that we would have better credibility as
> a Jewish organization if we were multi-issue rather than
> just, in effect, a Left or progressive Zionist organization.
> So we did have a plank in the platform but everybody
> felt that our specialization was the Middle East, and that's
> where we had our strength and that's why people were
> attracted to Breira. But I didn't agree. I thought it made
> us too easy to destroy. And there was another reason why
> it was easy to destroy Breira: it went for a "dissident elite"
> of establishment types who felt that Israel's policies were
> self-destructive. We had a number of prominent Ameri-
> can Jewish leaders, rabbis, editors, and intellectuals who
> were associated with us, but those people were very easy
> to pick off. They were more sensitive to criticism and
> they didn't have a grassroots behind them. My two main
> critiques of Breira and its ability to be effective were that
> it was too single issue and too elite in its organization.

NJA's grassroots base and multi-issue organizing laid a strong foundation to take controversial positions without being eviscerated like
Breira. New Jewish Agenda survived for a decade where other Jewish
groups calling for civil rights and nationhood for Palestinians (before
and since NJA) have been quickly pressured out of existence. While

---

17   Avi Rose, Letter about Re-Evaluation Counseling in NJA. http://newjewishagenda.word-
press.com/?attachment_id=180

this was certainly due to many factors, the impact of NJA's commitment to activism in the Jewish community as progressives and in the progressive community as Jews had a huge impact on NJA's ability to take strong critical stands without losing credibility. Though AFSI's Jean-Rael Isaac also wrote and published attack papers about New Jewish Agenda,[18] her attempt to discredit NJA was not as successful as the anti-Breira campaign. Gerry Serotta says, "NJA could not be killed no matter who tried to attack us. You couldn't kill NJA because we were part of the community."

Getting to Work

Following the Conference, equipped with a Unity Statement, By-Laws, an Interim Leadership Council, a national office, and about twenty local chapters, NJA began building the structures of an organization. Priority issues for the first year included:

- Reversing the trend toward nuclear proliferation
- Countering the right wing's attack on women's rights and other personal freedoms
- Reviewing Israel-Diaspora relationships in the wake of the recent Israeli elections
- Analyzing the Reagan socio-economic policies, concentrating on their impact on the cities and ties between Jews and other minorities
- Promoting a universal standard of human rights, especially in regard to the Jacobo Timerman controversy[19]
- Working to increase awareness of the needs of the Jewish disabled[20]

---

18 *The Anti-New Jewish Agenda* in 1987 and *New Jewish Agenda: Dissent or Disloyalty* in 1989
19 Jacobo Timerman was an Argentinian Jew who had been imprisoned by the military in 1977, tortured, and eventually forced into exile. His 1980 book documenting this experience, *Prisoner Without a Name, Cell Without a Number*, drew international attention from the Vatican and the Carter administration (among others). Timerman accused the Argentine military and government of anti-Semitism and likened them to Nazis, also denouncing Jewish leaders for ignoring the crisis. Timerman controversially denounced Reagan's support for the Argentinian regime and was attacked by conservative commentators who attempted to discredit his statements.
20 I found little documentation of NJA's disability activism in my research, but it is clear that the issue was a priority while not one of the main long-term Task Forces. I wonder if this work

- Developing a better understanding of the spiritual underpinnings of their work.[21]

While their organizing priorities shifted a bit over the coming years, many of NJA's long-term strategies were tested out early in the organization's development. In NJA, each task force coordinated work at the local and national level through Internal Discussion Bulletins[22], newsletters, conferences, and national task force gatherings. In a time before email, national task force members communicated through phone trees and hand-written letters, through mimeographed and photocopied mailings, and through face-to-face convening. Within many of the task forces, and occasionally outside of the task forces' wide subject areas, NJA members often established more focused Working Groups.

In their first year, NJA built shared consensus about their "spiritual underpinnings" through chapter events and mini-conferences. The Detroit chapter organized a large conference on "Being Jewish in the Eighties: A Renewed Commitment to Social Justice," which brought local and national speakers together, and the Bay Area Chapter held a one day workshop on disarmament.

Other chapters also got to work quickly, for example: Manhattan and Brooklyn protested in opposition to the annexation of the Golan Heights,[23] Northampton, MA mobilized to support exiled South African poet-activist Dennis Brutus in resisting deportation, Philadelphia protested against a Jewish organization honoring right-wing ex-mayor Frank Rizzo, and Boston Agenda's Labor Task Force joined efforts to improve conditions at a local hospital.

Early Campaign Evolution: Disarmament, Economic Justice, & Argentina's Anti-Semitism

Among NJA's National Task Forces, the Disarmament Task Force built national and local campaign work within months, and then made

---

took place largely at the local chapter level?

21   New Jewish Agenda, "Working Priorities" (Newsletter #8, Autumn 1981), 6.

22   NJA's strategy for promoting dialogue about heated issues

23   In December 1981, Israel passed the Golan Heights Law, applying Israeli law to Syrian territory in a move widely criticized by the international community.

especially powerful use of Jewish symbols and holy days in their political organizing. On August 9 1981, the Jewish holiday of Tisha B'Av
- which solemnly marks the destruction of the first Temple in Jeru-
salem[24] - coincided with the 36th anniversary of the atomic-bombing
of Nagasaki during WWII. NJA chapters held observances across the
country including protests, poetry, prayer, study, silent observance,
and chanting of Lamentations. In Chicago, one hundred people attended a service at KAM-Isaiah Israel synagogue and then marched to
the Museum of Science and Industry, chanting "Never Again. Never
Again Another Holocaust. Never Again Another Nagasaki." The
National NJA event was held in Washington, D.C.'s Lafayette Park. In
Seasons of our Joy, Rabbi Arthur Waskow remembers that "the occasion
was marked by a sizable number of Jews who undertook a traditional
observance of Tisha B'Av while being present near the White House
and the Soviet Embassy - buildings symbolic of the nuclear superpowers," thus marking the shared symbolism of the potential danger of world-destruction.[25] NJA released a statement with demands
including this one: "We call upon Jewish communities everywhere,
especially those in the United States and the Soviet Union, to throw
the whole weight of Jewish wisdom, energy, and creativity against the
nuclear arms race, against militarism and for meeting the needs and
hopes of the world's children."[26]

Also in August 1981, the Reagan Administration took bold anti-union
action against the Professional Air Traffic Controllers Union (PAT-
CO). When 12,500 members walked off their jobs in strike, Reagan
vowed to fire them all if they did not return to work within 48 hours.
A few days later, he made good on that promise. A few weeks later,
the AFL-CIO held a Solidarity Day march attended by half a million
people - union members and other progressive sectors - even bigger
than the 1968 march against Vietnam. NJA mobilized nationally for
this march and hit the streets as a visible Jewish block.
The issue list for 1981 references promoting a universal standard
of human rights, especially in regard to the Jacobo Timerman controversy, and the issue of human rights in Argentina was an early-
emerging NJA campaign. Argentina had been under military rule since
1976, and word had spread of over 15,000 citizens' disappearance and

---

24 In 586 BCE
25 Waskow, Rabbi Arthur. *Seasons of our Joy.* (Boston: Beacon Press, 1982)
26 Debra Orenstein, "Tisha B'Av - Nagasaki Day" (NJA Newsletter #8, Autumn 1981), 1.

thousands of political prisoners. A disproportionate number of those arrested were Jews, and many Argentinian Jews - including Timerman - reported brutal repression and torture with explicit anti-Semitic elements: Jewish prisoners were questioned about their religious affiliations and accused of plotting to seize sections of Argentina to set up a second Jewish state.

While the Carter administration had cut off military aid to Argentina, Reagan pushed for resumption of aid to the military junta. NJA resolved to make Argentinian anti-Semitism an organizing priority and established a letter-writing campaign for the release of Argentinian prisoners. NJA organized public education forums in Brooklyn, New Jersey, New Haven, and Boston. In San Francisco, the NJA Chapter co-sponsored a Purim party with an Argentinian group to benefit support work for Argentine political prisoners, reading the Megillah in Hebrew, English, and Spanish.

In early 1982, NJA was well positioned to bring together an interfaith coalition to challenge Reagan's war on the poor. On March 23rd 1982, the National Conference of Christians and Jews (NCCJ) presented President Reagan with the Charles Evans Hughes award for his "courageous leadership in governmental, civic, and humanitarian affairs" at a black tie event at the New York Hilton Hotel. That day, over 10,000[27] joined in protest of the award. The first event of the day-long protest was New Jewish Agenda's press conference of outraged Jewish and Christian clergy at the Stephen Wise Free Synagogue. *New York Amsterdam News* reported this statement:

> As Christians and Jews we condemn the Reagan policies of slashing spending on human needs, lavishing tax breaks on the very wealthy, starving education programs and creating wide-spread unemployment. Ronald Reagan's leadership has been disastrous for working people, racial minorities, women and especially the poor.[28]

---

27   Some estimates as high as 50,000
28   "10,000 Protesters Denounce Reagan" *New Amsterdam News: The New Black View.* (New York, NY), March 27, 1982.

That day, Chicago Rabbi Arnold Wolf returned his 1962 James Yard Brotherhood Award for civil rights activism to the NCCJ, stating that "If Reagan is a humanitarian, I am not."[29]

The Middle East Task Force and the Lebanon War

While New Jewish Agenda emphasized multi-issue organizing, the Middle East Task Force (METF) was always central to NJA's work. In a joint interview with NJA founder Rabbi Gerry Serotta and former NJA National Director/METF member Reena Bernards, both reflected that NJA had a historic and singular role to play, and that the METF was the most burning issue for Jews *as Jews*. Reena said, "There were other places to do social justice work [as Jews], but really no other place to express your desire for Israel/Palestine peace. Friends of Peace Now was getting organized right around the same time, but they were much more cautious, because their Israeli partners kept them cautious. It's like that now, too." Serotta added, "They were single-issue, and directed by the Israeli peace movement. Agenda was the only place since Breira had died for criticism from the Diaspora."

Between the end of Breira and the beginning of New Jewish Agenda, Jewish activism around Israel/Palestine had continued, and NJA joined a field that was still deeply controversial and heated within the Jewish community. Gordon Fellman, co-chair of the METF for five years (1982-1987), remembered that the mission-tension within NJA as a whole was also very present in the METF:

> Our task in the METF was to persuade Jews not to
> be anti-Arab racists and to persuade Leftists not to be
> anti-Israel rejectionists. I found that kind of exciting, a
> challenge because nobody else was doing that at the time.
> Within Agenda were people who wanted to give up on
> the Jewish community and stand firmly with the Left.
> I, and a number of others, thought that was a mistake;
> we should really be working in the Jewish community to
> change consciousness as well as on the Left. We went
> through this over and over again.

---

29   Freeman, Kevin. "Reagan Denounces the 'obscenity of Anti-semitism and Racism' and Reaffirms U.S. Commitment to Israel." *Jewish Telegraphic Agency*, Mar 25 1982.

As National Task Forces were still establishing their goals and structures, NJA was called to respond to the onset of the June 6, 1982 Lebanon War. Israeli Defense Forces, under direction of then-Defense Minister Ariel Sharon[30], invaded Lebanon into Beirut, expelling the PLO and occupying the area[31]. This action was wide rejected by the international community. NJA was the only American Jewish organization that clearly opposed the war in Lebanon from its onset, and the Middle East Task Force stepped up its actions.

Local chapters were able to mobilize the most immediate responses, including a public statement by NJA's Washington DC area chapter two days after the invasion, a statement and protest vigil by Massachusetts chapter *Khevre*, a City Hall protest by Philadelphia NJA, a major "Call for Peace" and memorial service in Detroit with a speaker from Israel's Peace Now movement, and a town meeting in Boston with featured speakers including foreign policy experts Noam Chomsky and Irene Gendzier, as well as NJA's own Gordon Fellman. On June 30th, New Jewish Agenda National published a full-page ad in the *New York Times* denouncing the Israeli invasion of Lebanon politically and spiritually, signed by the entire membership of NJA including more than 40 U.S. rabbis. The same ad was also published on July 2nd in the *Jewish Post and Opinion*.

The Task Force next initiated a petition campaign calling for endorsement of "The Paris Declaration", a groundbreaking statement by three international Jewish leaders[32]. The petition read:

> Peace need not be made between friends, but between
> enemies who have struggled and suffered. Our sense of
> Jewish history and the moral imperatives of this moment
> require us to insist that the time is urgent for mutual
> recognition between Israel and the Palestinian people.
> There must be a stop to the sterile debate, whereby the
> Arab world challenges the existence of Israel and Jews

---

30   Sharon was later elected as Israel's Prime Minister, serving from 2001-2006
31   This military action followed a number of PLO attacks against Israel including terrorist attacks and rocket fire against Northern Israel.
32   Dr. Nahum Goldmann, Former President of the World Zionist Organization, Founder-President of the World Jewish Congress; Philip M. Klutznick, Former U.S. Secretary of Commerce, President Emeritus of the World Jewish Congress, Honorary President of B'nai B'rith International; and Pierre Mendes France, Former Prime Minister of France.

challenge the political legitimacy of the Palestinian fight
for independence.

The real issue is not whether Palestinians are entitled to
their rights, but how to bring this about while ensuring Israel's security and regional stability. Ambiguous concepts
such as "autonomy" are no longer sufficient, for they too
often are used to confuse rather than to clarify. Needed
now is the determination to reach a political accommoda-
tion between Israeli and Palestinian nationalisms.

The war in Lebanon must stop. Israel must lift its siege
of Beirut in order to facilitate negotiations with the PLO,
leading to a political settlement. Mutual recognition must
be vigorously pursued. And there should be negotiations
with the aim of achieving co-existence between the Israeli
and Palestinian peoples based on self-determination.[33]

The Middle East Task Force also utilized the strategy of public
protest, including a protest against Israeli Prime Minister Menachem
Begin when he spoke in Los Angeles that year.

The Lebanon War was a watershed moment that entirely changed the
political landscape for American Jewish peace activists. Whereas Breira
was founded shortly before the Yom Kippur War which received
major support from American Jews, the Lebanon Invasion exposed
the silencing of dissent by American Jewish leaders.[34] The resulting
cultural climate afforded more opportunities for criticism of Israel
within the Jewish community.

Next-generation activist Avi Rosenblit, who went on to direct D.C.'s
Jews United for Justice, wrote a senior thesis titled "New Jewish Agenda and the Lebanon War." He explains,

---

33 New Jewish Agenda, "Call for a West Bank Settlement Freeze" (Newsletter #12, Spring
1983), 1 and insert.

34 This was especially clear in relation to the September 1982 Sabra and Shatilla Massacres
in which Lebanese Christian Militia members killed Palestinian civilians in two Beirut refugee
camps. An Israeli Investigative Commission found Ariel Sharon personally responsible and he
was forced to resign as Defense Minister.

American Jews never approached a consensus on the issue of Israeli settlements in the West Bank and the Gaza Strip, and during the Lebanon War [the American Jewish community] was evenly divided on whether or not to withdraw from these areas. Polls of the Jewish community in the early 1980s illustrate that settlements were not the only issue on which they had strong, divergent, and critical opinions. Specifically during the war in Lebanon, American Jews responded less favorably to Israeli policy than they had at any time in Israel's history.[35]

To be sure, though, NJA's analysis was not appreciated in many parts of the Jewish community. Perhaps the most extreme example of irate response to NJA's organizing about Lebanon was the widely publicized mass excommunication of all NJA members, performed by three rabbis in a Holiday Inn in Tewksbury, Massachusetts. For the traitorous acts of supporting Palestinian rights and also for recognizing the rights of Gay and Lesbian Jews, the rabbis performed such ancient rites as blowing a ram's horn and snuffing candles to represent the end of the targets' spiritual lives. In addition to NJA members, they also excommunicated Nobel Laureate Salvador Luria and Noam Chomsky.

The Task Force on Developing a Progressive Jewish World View had worked for a year to organize a June 1982 Conference outside of Philadelphia. There, fifty members joined for a weekend to formulate shared philosophy and look at some of the practical questions that arise when organizing with both secular and religious Jews: Should they link actions to religious events? Should they march on Shabbat? The gathering included representatives from each local chapter as well as a number of members invited because of their specific knowledge in fields of Jewish religion, Yiddish culture, secularism, feminism, leftist politics, and psychology. Planners included Arthur Waskow, well-known secularist Max Rosenfeld, Larry Bush of the secular progressive *Jewish Currents* Magazine, and Nancy Fuchs-Kreimer of the Reconstructionist Rabbinical School.

---

35   Avi Daniel Rosenblit. "*The New Jewish Agenda and the Lebanon War: Negotiating a discourse in pro-Israel American Jewish identity, 1980-1983*" (Undergraduate Honors Thesis. Northwestern University, 2003), 7.

As it turned out, this conference was held during the first weeks of the invasion of Lebanon, and attendee Richard Silverstein stated that "the consternation and outrage felt by all of the participants toward these events created an underlying tension amidst all the weekend's proceedings.[36]" Indeed, an NJA statement on the Lebanon invasion was drafted at the conference. Despite some participants' distraction, the work of the conference continued and reported lively discussions and panels.

Massive Disarmament Mobilization and a Nuclear Freeze Petition

In June 1982, the UN held a Special Session on Disarmament. Mobilization for Survival and other groups scheduled a June 12th mass demonstration and march in New York, as well as a week of workshops and activities leading up to the rally. NJA Member Bob Trachtenberg reflected on the power of the political moment in his NJA Newsletter article, "Disarmament":

> People all over the world are recognizing that the nuclear arms race is the greatest danger to the continuation of life on the planet. The present US administration has fired people's fears by reviving the concept of a winnable nuclear war.
>
> The effort to stop the nuclear arms race is being organized by local, grassroots groups. People who do not usually view themselves as able to affect global issues are finding outlets for their concern.[37]

NJA sat on the national coordinating body for the demo, and mobilized nationally to bring members to the march as well as to solidarity marches in LA and San Francisco. The night before the demonstration, NJA sponsored a "Sabbath of Peace" event with Jewish Peace Fellowship and the Stephen Wise Free Synagogue. Rabbi Lynn Gotlieb led the service, followed by potluck dinner, Sephardic and

---

36   In Joyce Bresler, "Toward a Progressive World View" (NJA Newsletter#10, Summer 1982),5.

37   Bob Trachtenberg, "Disarmament" (NJA Newsletter # 9, Spring 1981), 1.

Ashkenazi music, poetry by Yuri Suhl, and a talk on Judaism and civil disobedience by peace activist Sharon Kleinman. On June 12th, NJA took to the streets joined by a number of other Jewish organizations, marching with banners and signs in Hebrew, English, and Yiddish. The March took place on a Saturday, so arrangements had to be made to host Shabbat-observant visitors so they could walk to the demo. Several hundred NJA members joined with an estimated crowd of one million people marching on June 12th, at that time the largest Disarmament Rally in American history.[38]

Following the Rally, a Nuclear Freeze campaign was the next big strategy. The Freeze campaign was endorsed at city government and state legislation levels across the country. Voters approved a Nuclear Freeze in nine states out of ten on 1982 ballots, and it would go on to pass the House of Representatives in 1983. New Jewish Agenda brought a Nuclear Freeze resolution to an equivalent high-level establishment body in the American Jewish world, the Council of Jewish Foundations (CJF). There, at the November 1982 CJF General Assembly, NJA lobbying met with huge success as they passed a resolution calling for passage of a multi-lateral nuclear arms freeze. The General Assembly CJF resolution had a powerful ripple effect in the larger Jewish community, prompting other major Jewish organizations, such as the American Jewish Congress, B'nai Brith and the National Jewish Community Relations Council, to issue similar statements.

NJA's Disarmament Task Force was very active and well-networked, but they did face barriers due to their association with the Middle East Task Force. In 1983, Arthur Waskow formed The Shalom Center, another organization with a focus on peace and anti-nuclear activism from a Jewish perspective. Jeffrey Dekro (an early leader in both NJA and the Shalom Center) reflected that Shalom Center's formation was due at least in part to the fact that NJA couldn't receive full funding to do disarmament work because of their high profile and controversial work on Israel. The Shalom Center and NJA's Task Force worked closely together, and the Shalom Center continued disarmament work long after NJA shut down.

---

38 "The biggest demonstration on earth until the global anti-Iraq war march of Feb 15 2003" http://www.icanw.org/1982

Attacks from the Right, and Internal Impacts

The Summer 1982 NJA Newsletter reported a campaign of right-wing attack against NJA reminiscent of the tactics of the FBI's Cointel-pro program used to disrupt many social movements including the Black Panther Party. Three unsigned letters printed on pro-Palestinian organizations' letterhead were circulated among Jewish organizations across the country, claiming that the pro-Palestinian organizations were in contact with NJA leadership and urging "all friends of the Palestinian revolution" to support NJA. The letters also included inflammatory statements such as, "If we can exploit and encourage such (American Jewish criticism of Israel), we can further isolate and undermine the Zionist regime." At the same time, racist right-wing Jewish Defense League (JDL) founder Meir Kahane[39] publicized one of the letters in Israel, and the JDL purchased a full-page ad in the Detroit News to reprint the text of that letter.

The NJA Newsletter declares: "THESE LETTERS ARE PATENT FRAUDS. One of the organizations in question has been defunct for four years,[40] and the other has vehemently denied sending any such letter." NJA filed a mail fraud complaint and put out a statement and press release explaining that NJA was being targeted because of criticism of specific Israeli policies. In fact, this smear attempt provided an opportunity for NJA to spread the word on their real, and nuanced, political positions. Their press release was picked up by many Jewish newspapers.[41]

While this attack was relatively ineffective in thwarting NJA's work, it foretold of more to come – and it triggered anxious concerns from those who witnessed the destruction of Breira. The same 1982 NJA Newsletter included a section about Chapter Autonomy with reflections on a recent controversy. In June 1982, at the time of the Israeli invasion of Lebanon, the Manhattan NJA Chapter voted to endorse and send a speaker to a rally in coalition with Palestinian groups and others in front of the Israeli embassy. Members of the National Steer-

39   Meir Kahane founded the JDL in 1968 in the United States, and the Israeli Kach political party, which advocated expulsion of all Palestinians.
40   This refers to the U.S. Ad-Hoc Committee for Palestinian Rights.
41   New Jewish Agenda, "NJA Confronts Attacks from the Right" (Newsletter #10, Summer 1982), 3.

ing Committee pressured the Manhattan Chapter to drop out of the event, expressing concern for the growth and survival of NJA and their broad coalition work. Special concern was expressed about the Manhattan Chapter's high visibility to media and other Jewish organizations' headquarters. National Steering Committee members went as far as threatening expulsion, and the Manhattan Chapter did withdraw from the coalition. The Newsletter article reports that this pressure "was blatantly inappropriate and not in accordance with our by-laws and democratic process." A meeting about this process resulted in a letter of apology from National Steering Committee members, and a larger conversation about future processes. The article clarified the autonomy of Chapters, while urging communication with the National Steering Committee – especially on Middle East issues.[42]

National Platform Adopted

At the November 1982 Delegates Conference in NYC, sixty-five elected representatives of NJA chapters and at-large members from across the US accepted their first National Platform. Their statement explained that, "The platform represents the climax of an extensive cooperative process that began at Agenda's founding conference in 1980. It represents our current political analysis with respect to the major issues of the day. We anticipate that it will be revised and amended as needed in the years to come." The Platform, reprinted in this book, included a general Statement of Purpose and specific statements on eighteen issue areas including "Women in the Work Force, Family, and Reproductive Rights," and "Relations Between Israel and North American Jewry.[43]"

Sanctuary for Central American Refugees

While much of American Jewry's attention was focused on the Middle East, NJA was also getting activated in the Sanctuary Movement, which provided refuge for Central Americans fleeing political repression and state violence including government and paramilitary death

---

42   New Jewish Agenda, "Perspectives on 'Chapter Autonomy'" (Newsletter #10, Summer 1982), 3.
43   Included in this volume, see Appendix III.

squads in Guatemala and El Salvador. The murders of Archbishop Oscar Romero and four U.S. churchwomen in El Salvador had increased visibility to many in the U.S., and it grew clear that the Reagan administration was not only refusing asylum to Central American refugees, but also actively funding the brutal militaries that were perpetrating these human rights atrocities.

Initially, the Sanctuary Movement had been a group of progressive churches inspired by the Christian Liberation Theology movement. In winter of 1982, the Milwaukee chapter of NJA was asked to find a prominent Jewish community leader to speak at a vigil supporting local refugees. This led to a local congregation, Emanu-El B'nai Jeshurun, becoming the first synagogue to join the Sanctuary movement by providing financial and legal resources for a family of Salvadoran refugees. NJA distributed educational packets on the issues to over 2,000 rabbis and synagogues and published articles and letters to the editor. In less than a year, over twenty synagogues were active in the Sanctuary Movement.

Organizing for a Settlement Freeze

Following up on their petition campaign during the Lebanon War and their successful work on the Nuclear Freeze campaign, in 1983 NJA initiated a new campaign for a freeze on Israeli Settlements in the West Bank. First, NJA circulated a petition ultimately signed by 5,000 American Jews which enabled a public education campaign about the effects of settlement policies on the Middle East peace process. The petition read:

> We are American Jews committed to the security and well being of Israel. We join with the peace forces in Israel who call for a freeze of Jewish settlement activity in the West Bank, and who oppose all actions by the Israeli government designed to incorporate the West Bank and its population into the State of Israel.

> We believe that a negotiated exchange of territory for peace will contribute to Israel's long-term security, enhance its democratic character and promote justice for

Israelis, Palestinians and all others who have suffered through this painful conflict.[44]

The METF led an intensive political study mission to Israel and the Occupied Territories in the summer of 1983, meeting with academics, journalists and leading political figures.

Next, in November 1983, NJA made a bold move: they brought the Settlement Freeze petition to the General Assembly of the Council of Jewish Federations (CJF)[45]. Rabbi Gerry Serotta explained the power of this campaign decision:

> The Council of Jewish Federations is really the heart of the establishment; it raises most of the money in the Jewish community. They rarely take political resolutions, but they have discussions when they have an annual meeting, when it's like the entire organized Jewish community is there! You have to bring a resolution through a local federation. Well, [an NJA member's] father was a major giver in Minneapolis, so the Minneapolis/St. Paul federation brought a resolution that said "We think the American Jewish community should recommend to the state of Israel a freeze on settlements on the West Bank."[46] This was in 1983! The fact that we got it on the floor was a tremendous victory and it was reported widely that the Jewish community is considering this thing. It was tabled after some discussion, not defeated. We brought Haim Ramon to the CJF meeting. He was the youngest member of the Labor party in the Knesset at the time and a very outspoken dove, so we brought dovish politics into the heart of the establishment, successfully! We were a far-left gadfly, but we were part of the community.

---

44   New Jewish Agenda, "Call for a West Bank Settlement Freeze," Newsletter #12, Spring 1983: 1 and insert.

45   A year earlier, NJA had successfully brought and passed a Nuclear Freeze petition at the Council of Jewish Federation. This set a precedent for presenting the more controversial petition.

46   A *Jewish Telegraphic Agency* article reports that the resolution stated: "Israel could build on the gains it made at Camp David by refraining from actions such as the construction of settlements which lead toward the incorporation of the West Bank into Israel proper." Murray Zuckoff, "At the GA of the CJF: Resolution on the Mideast Emphasizes Importance of U.S.-Israel Being in Accord," *Jewish Telegraphic Agency*, Nov 23 1983.

NJA successfully brought the conversation about unethical Israeli settlement expansion to the General Assembly of the Council of Jewish Federations and into the court of public opinion. Although the resolution was tabled, this was a huge win. Christie Balka remembers that this success reflected the power of NJA's diversity and resulting unpredictability:

> We were there to act like nice boys and girls and organize quietly among delegates. You have to understand, this was one of the first times I'd shaved my legs! But they were scared to death that we were going to sit-in or do guerrilla theater... It shows that if you can appear unpredictable, you have more strength than your numbers would predict.

Though the Settlement resolution was tabled, another resolution on the Middle East - this one largely focused on criticizing Arab nations-was influenced to include a rare statement acknowledging Israel's shared responsibility for creating conditions for peace: "All parties need to be flexible and open in terms of the negotiated process and not preclude any options that lead to peace."[47]

March on Washington for Jobs, Peace, and Freedom

August 1983 brought the 20th anniversary of the 1963 "Great March on Washington," perhaps best known as the site of Rev. Martin Luther King Jr's "I Have a Dream" speech. An estimated 8,000 Jews had attended the 1963 march, including speakers Rabbi Uri Miller, President of the Synagogue Council of America and Rabbi Joachim Prinz, President of the American Jewish Congress.

Mainstream Jewish organizations objected to the initial call for a 20th Anniversary March, concerned that the messaging included an anti-Israel focus. Another barrier to Jewish involvement, the March would take place on a Saturday, the Sabbath. When most mainstream Jewish groups refused to join the 1983 organizing, New Jewish Agenda ended up as one of only two national Jewish organizations that mobilized widely for the march, along with the the Union of American Hebrew

---

47   Zuckoff, "At the GA of the CJF," 1983.

Congregations (UAHC). Smaller groups also joined the march, including the Jewish Bund (secular socialist labor group), D.C.-area Jews for an Israeli-Palestinian Peace, Jewish humanist congregation Beth Chai and the Fabrengen chavurah. Despite the absence of more mainstream groups, the large Jewish contingent marching with a 24-foot banner that read "Justice, Justice Thou Shall Pursue", and a large Jewish star with the word "Shalom" created an important opportunity to build bridges and demonstrate Jewish commitment to the weekend's themes. In fact, according to a *Jewish Week* article about the march, only one speaker out of seventy – a representative of the American Indian Movement – used the opportunity to criticize Israel.[48]

NJA also organized a Shabbat service and celebration in the Marvin Center ballroom of George Washington University, bringing together over 500 people. The Shabbat gathering, organized by NJA's Philadelphia Chapter and led by Rabbi Devora Bartnoff, blended religious and secular observance, included speeches by Martin Luther King III and Susannah Heschel, whose father Rabbi Abraham Joshua Heschel had been a close comrade of MLK. The UAHC also organized a Shabbat event, with speakers including MLK's widow, Coretta Scott King.

Organizing around the Jewish Holidays: Passover, Sukkot, and Hanukah

NJA's earliest organizing included events tied to Jewish Holidays such as the Tisha B'av/Nagasaki Commemoration. This progressive organizing model was not invented by NJA, but they made good use of the strategy across their Task Forces.

In Spring 1984, NJA published *The Shalom Seders: Three Haggadahs* for Passover. One of the haggadahs, *The Rainbow Seder* by Arthur Waskow, focused on environmental and nuclear disarmament concerns. In an introduction to the book, Waskow explained that this seder was the fifth reincarnation of his 1969 *Freedom Seder*, which brought the exodus story together with the struggles of modern liberation movements in the aftermath of the assassination of Martin Luther King, Jr. Waskow described how this new incarnation of the Seder came from

---

48 "March Called a Success." *Jewish Week of Maryland, Virginia and Washington DC*, Sept 1-7,1983.

his own evolution through the Jewish Renewal movement and the Rainbow Sign project, which worked against world nuclear holocaust from a Jewish perspective.

Second, the *Seder of the Children of Abraham* by the Philadelphia NJA chapter, called for peace between Israelis and Palestinians. Waskow explained of authors Devorah Bartnoff, Catherine Essoyan. Mordechai Liebling, and Brian Walt, "What they accomplished was a remarkable transformation in the Haggadah. Pharoah was transformed into the endless, oppressive war between the two peoples – liberation into the need for hope for both peoples to make a decent peace with one another."

The *Haggadah of Liberation*, the third in the series contributed by the Seattle NJA Chapter/Kadima. The origins of this Seder began in 1971 with a Jewish women's group in Portland, OR who wrote a new Haggadah together on rice paper to tell the story from a women's liberation perspective. This rice-paper Hagaddah traveled to Brooklyn with Bria Chakofsky, then back west to Seattle and Kadima. After a few years of evolution in Kadima's Cultural Committee, it joined this New Jewish Agenda publication.[49]

That fall, NJA chapters sponsored both "Sukkat Shalom, Shelter of Peace" and Rainbow Sign celebrations across the country, linking traditional observances with the call for nuclear disarmament. NJA also joined eight other national Jewish organizations in building a sukkah in Lafayette Park across from the White House to draw attention to anti-nuclear organizing, building on the momentum of the nuclear freeze resolutions across the country.

A *Jewish Telegraphic Agency* article quotes Theodore Mann, president of the American Jewish Congress in a statement at the Lafayette Park protest:

> As Jews who sadly know better than most about the human vulnerability symbolized by the Succah, we must send a message. First to our own Jewish leaders and to Jews in communities and on campuses throughout America... Then altogether, we must convince America's

---

49   New Jewish Agenda. *The Shalom Seders: Three Haggadahs.* (New York: Adama Books, 1984.)

leaders and the whole public that this nation's single most
important responsibility is to build a structure of peace, a
Succat Shalom.

In that same article, NJA spokespeople added that the Jewish gathering includes a focus on poverty, and the relationship between funding for nuclear arms and the defunding of social services.[50]

Then, on the last night of Hanukah 1984 (also Christmas Day), NJA sponsored protests outside South African consulates in five U.S. cities, which received international press attention. In New York, four protesters were arrested in an NJA demonstration outside the South African Consulate. In Washington, three hundred members of New Jewish Agenda and a number of more mainstream organizations came to the consulate to protest. In a press statement, NJA explained: "This effort will permit Christian supporters of the Free South Africa movement the opportunity to spend the day with family and friends while sending the South African government the clear message that the struggle against their racist, apartheid policies will not cease even for a single day."[51]

Tours for Internal and Public Education: Israel/Palestine and Central America

NJA's Middle East Task Force organized many speaking tours to spread the word about a range of Israeli, American, and Palestinian peace movements working together in solidarity. This offered American Jews a way to understand critiques of Israel outside of the simplistic mainstream narrative of "self-hating Jews." In the Summer of 1984, the Middle East Task Force sent a second political study mission to Israel and the Occupied Territories.

The same year, NJA and the (Quaker) American Friends Service Committee (AFSC) co-sponsored a national speaking tour featuring Peace Now leader Mordechai Bar-on, former Israeli Defense Force (IDF)

50   David Friedman, "At a Succah in Washington: Several Hundred People Rally to Protest Against the Funding, Development,." *Jewish Telegraphic Agency,* Oct 15 1984.
51   "250-300 Jewish Protesters Relieve Christian Colleagues at Rally Against Apartheid in South Africa." *Jewish Telegraphic Agency,* Dec 271984.

officer and member of Israeli Knesset, and Mohammed Milhem, deposed West Bank Palestinian Mayor. These speaking tour dialogues were followed by local discussions between American Jewish and Arab communities and resulted in PBS television special, "The Arab and the Israeli."

Also in 1984, NJA coordinated a 26-city tour by Dov Yermiya, the oldest reservist in the IDF and a civil rights and anti-racist activist in Israel, with Palestinian Munir Fasheh.

In another example of internal-education programming with a public-education outcome, NJA sponsored a 1984 delegation of national Jewish leaders to Nicaragua to investigate human rights conditions. At the time, the Reagan administration was spreading allegations of anti-Semitism by the Sandanista government, a bold attempt to garner American Jewish voters' support for U.S. aid to armed rebel groups opposing the Sandanistas, known as the "Contras." We now know that Reagan was secretly funding the Contras between 1984-1986, against explicit Congressional ruling, in what came to be known as the "Iran-Contra" scandal.

NJA's fact-finding delegation included Rabbi Marshall T. Meyer, who Gerry Serotta described as "a real hero of the Latin American Jewish community for standing up to the Argentine junta. He was in Argentina for 25 years so he had tremendous credibility."

The delegation returned with a report that the Sandanistas were not engaging in anti-Semitic behavior or policies, and in fact that Nicaragua was willing to resume diplomatic talks with Israel and to oppose any forms of anti-Semitism. Through widespread publicity, the 1984 delegation contributed to discrediting the Reagan administration's attempts to garner American Jewish community support for the Contras. NJA sent many more delegations to Central America, and joined with other peace groups for lobbying and speaking against U.S. aid to the Contras. They also represented the Jewish community in the Pledge of Resistance coalition and the Inter-Religious Task Force on Central America.

NJA also distributed two brochures. One, "Jews and Central America: The Need to Act," provided political, military, and economic analysis that addressed the situation in the region, including Israel's role as a supplier of arms to repressive regimes, and concerns that kept progressive Jews from responding to the Central American crisis.[52] The second pamphlet, "Jews and the Sanctuary Movement" offered historical connection and scriptural commandments obligating Jews to harbor the persecuted and protect them from harm, and a list of ways to help.[53]

In 1986, Agenda sponsored national speaking tours by three rabbis whose congregations had offered sanctuary to Central American refugees. Agenda's "Jewish Witness for Peace" delegation created a 30-minute video called "Crossing Borders" which was distributed within the Jewish community as an educational tool.

NJA's Feminist Task Force: The Personal is Political

Jewish Feminist leadership was part of NJA's culture from its earliest days, though prior to 1985 the majority of NJA's feminist programming seems to have taken place at the chapter level. A well-attended October 1984 Conference on Women and Judaism organized by the DC Chapter of NJA (WANJA) is one example. Another is an early 1985 WANJA meeting on the theme "What do we mean by a Jewish feminist perspective?"

There were strong Jewish feminist and lesbian movements evolving at the time of NJA's founding, but they had little cross-pollination during NJA's early years. Clare Kinberg, who organized the National Convention in Ann Arbor in the summer of 1985, explained:

> I wanted to connect where I was coming from with what
> NJA was doing... On the local scene, every city had a Jew-
> ish lesbian group and seders and stuff going on, but not
> very many of the people were involved in NJA. Agenda
> was seen as more mainstream because they wanted to or-
> ganize among American Jews. It felt like two trains going

52   NJA, "Jews and Central America, The Need to Act." Pamphlet. http://newjewishagenda. wordpress.com/?attachment_id=183
53   NJA, "Jews and the Sanctuary Movement." Pamphlet. http://newjewishagenda.wordpress. com/?attachment_id=178

on separate tracks to me, and I really wanted to combine them. That was a vision that I made for the '85 National Conference. I strategized to invite Adrienne Rich and Elly Bulkin and other people, who were prominent among Jewish lesbians as writers and activists and leaders, to the convention... A lot of lesbian feminists got involved at that convention and afterwards.

The 1985 Conference passed a resolution to begin a Feminist Task Force (FTF). The national FTF encouraged local chapters to form Feminist Task Forces, as well, and work on recruiting women who would be interested in that work to NJA.

In her article "Challenges of Difference at *Bridges*," Kinberg wrote about the impact of Jewish feminists on NJA:

> Feminists brought to NJA what we had learned from Feminist organizing. We initiated structural changes with the organization, including gender parity in all national leadership bodies, guaranteed "out" lesbian/gay represen-tation in governance, and men's and women's caucuses. NJA's structure also insisted on geographic diversity (within the continental United States) and representation of people over age fifty-five. NJA, formulaically at least, applied a central insight of the feminist movement: the realities and contexts of our personal lives are inseparable from our political perspectives and actions."[54]

New Jewish Agenda's Feminist Task Force was also heavily influenced by the work of many feminists of color who had been challenging the white-dominated culture of the larger feminist movement, and making space for complicated conversations about overlapping identities. In her book *Yours in Struggle*, Elly Bulkin (an FTF member) wrote:

> Much as the women's movement of the late Sixties and early Seventies had its roots in the earlier civil rights struggle and the New Left, both the increasing number of women who define ourselves as *Jewish* feminists and

---

54   Clare Kinberg. "The Challenge of Difference at Bridges," in *The Narrow Bridge: Jewish Views on Multiculturalism*. ed. Marla Brettschneider (New Brunswick, NJ: Rutgers Univ Press, 1996). 29.

our growing activism against anti-Semitism within and
outside the women's community owe a significant debt as
well to the emergence in the last decade of a broad-base
Third World feminist movement in this country. Women
of color, especially lesbians, have been in the forefront of
creating theory and practice that insist on the important
of differences among women and on the positive aspects
of cultures and identities. With "identity politics" as a
basis, feminists of color have been able to link analysis
with day-to-day political activism, as they lay out a range
of ways in which individual and institutional oppression
works.[55]

The work of the FTF overlapped with many of the other campaigns:
anti-racist organizing, Middle-East peace, and economic justice were
among the FTF's biggest focuses. NJA's Feminist Task Force housed
both the Gay/Lesbian Working Group and (later) the AIDS Working
Group, perhaps because the FTF's membership was infused by the
evolving Jewish lesbian community.

The UN Decade for Women Forum

In 1985, NJA sent a delegation from the Feminist Task Force to
Nairobi, Kenya, to attend the UN Decade for Women Non-Governmental Organization's (NGO) Forum. This NGO Forum gathered
over 14,000 representatives while the simultaneous official Decade for
Women Forum was attended by 2,000 government representatives.
NJA's delegation, including Executive Director Reena Bernards and
National Co-Chair Christie Balka, presented a successful dialogue at
the NGO Forum that had been organized collaboratively over many
months between feminist Jewish, African-American, and Arab[56] activists, and changed the tone of a major conversation at the Forums.

55   Elly Bulkin, Minnie Bruce Pratt, and Barbara Smith. *Yours in Struggle: Three Feminist Perspectives on Antisemitism and Racism.* (Ithaca, NY. Firebrand Books, 1988), 98.
56   It is worth noting that many people are Arab and Jewish, or African-American and Jewish
, and these overlapping identities can be made invisible by naming these groups as separate and
conflicting communities. Where I use these distinctions, I mean to name – as NJA did – the
primary identities that people are representing in coalition work, and not to dismiss Sephardim,
Mizrahim, other Jews of Color, or multicultural or multiracial Jews. For more information on
Jewish racial diversity, check out www.jewishmultiracialnetwork.org/ and Melanie Kaye/Kan-
trowitz's important book *The Colors of Jews: Racial Politics and Radical Diasporism* (2007).

The UN Decade for Women Forum began in 1975 in Mexico City, followed by a 1980 Forum in Copenhagen. In 1975, a "Zionism equals Racism" resolution had passed the UN Forum, to the dismay of Jewish and Israeli feminists. This was the first time such a resolution had passed within a UN body – soon followed by a similar resolution at the UN General Assembly. The 1980 Forum was reportedly disastrous, with Palestinian-Jewish tensions and raging disputes interrupting participants from building consensus on any other issues. Palestinian representatives and those from other Arab nations denied Israel's right to exist, and Jewish women reported widespread verbal abuse and anti-Semitism. Jewish representatives responded by rejecting the inclusion of Palestinians in the Forum and attempting to silence the voices of any who expressed criticism of Israel.

Members of NJA returned from the Copenhagen forum with clear intention to do the coalition-building work necessary to shift the conversation. To that end, they convened three NYC meetings between Arab, Jewish, Black, and other feminist leaders. Yet, this successful campaign was not without growing pains. A letter of critique from Carol Haddad, a representative of the Feminist Arab Network, to NJA's Feminist Task Force, identified and challenged the ways that NJA organizers had invited African-American and Arab feminists to the table late in the process, and had tightly controlled the conversation. The letter criticizes one Jewish dialogue organizer's anti-Arab racism in a recent article, and generally questions whether the Jewish women offering an invitation to dialogue are committed to really addressing anti-Arab racism or simply seeking "dialogue for the sake of dialogue."[57] The letter illustrates the necessity of NJA's ongoing work to address internal community issues of white privilege and racism, in addition to their external work to challenge anti-Semitism.
In Nairobi, Balka and Bernards attended daily Jewish caucus meetings at a Nairobi synagogue, formed a caucus with Peace Now, and attended numerous workshops on Middle East topics. They distributed 4,000 copies of the NJA brochure offering guidelines for the dialogue, including these two:

- Israel will not be singled out as a unique violator of human rights. Nor will the Palestine Liberation Or-

57 Carol Haddad, (Letter, July 1 1985). (online at http://newjewishagenda.wordpress.com/?attachment_id=174)

ganization be singled out as a terrorist organization.
Standards for human rights and international conduct
should be applied uniformly to all countries.

- The equating of Zionism with racism is divisive and
  inaccurate. Zionism is a multi-faceted movement for
  Jewish national liberation and it is therefore uncon-
  structive to the process of dialogue to assert that it is
  equivalent with racism. (This is not to deny that racist
  policies do exist within Israel.) It is in the interest of
  all women including Palestinians that the issue not be
  addressed in this way.

NJA held a major public workshop at the NGO Forum, "Israeli and
Palestinian Women in Dialogue: A Search for Peace," with speakers
Mary Khass and Lisa Blum. According to a year-end report on the
collaborative dialogue, "[Speakers] shared their mutual concerns over
the continuing hostilities, the impact of violence on their respective
communities, and the need for mutual recognition and self-determination for both the Jewish and Palestinian people." Balka is quoted in a
Kansas City Jewish Chronicle article saying that this was the best-attended
workshop at the NGO Forum, and it was translated into five lan-
guages.[58] NJA also coordinated two off-the-record meetings between
Israeli, Palestinian, Egyptian, Arab-American, European Jewish and
American Jewish women.

The "Zionism = Racism" declaration was again brought to the UN
Forum in 1985, proposed by the Soviet Union and supported by Iran
and Syria. The language was struck down in large part due to Kenya's
peacemaking negotiations. In the paragraph in question, "Zionism"
was replaced by "and all other forms of racism," language that eventually passed by consensus including representatives from the Soviet
Union and the Palestinian Liberation Organization.

This was a big victory for NJA – they had played a crucial role in shifting a deadlocked conversation towards dialogue, with international
impact. An NJA Press Release quotes Christie Balka: "Many of us are
committed to continuing these discussions now that the conference in

---

58   Michael Deverey, "Defeat of Racism Resolution Seen as 'Victory,'" *The Kansas City Jewish Chronicle*, Nov 15, 1985.

Nairobi is over. I found a hunger for contact on all sides. New Jewish Agenda intends to persist in the dialogue."[59] After the 1985 Forum, NJA attendees spoke around the country about the process and outcomes of their organizing.

Up Against the JDL Again, LA

In 1985, NJA joined protests in solidarity against violent anti-Arab attacks in Los Angeles. That year, a series of attacks against LA's Arab community, believed to be the work of the Jewish Defense League (JDL), culminated in the tragic assassination of Alex Odeh, Director of the American Arab Anti-Discrimination Committee's Southern CA office.

Alex Odeh's murder brought NJA into direct conflict with racist right-wing terrorists in the JDL. Richard Silverstein, then regional director for New Jewish Agenda in Los Angeles, has written about this experience on his blog, "*Tikun Olam*,"[60]

> The local NJA chapter took out an ad in the Los Angeles Jewish Journal mourning Alex's death and calling for Jews to commit themselves to the ideals for reconciliation he represented. After his death, Agenda held a December, 1985 Hanukah party and invited Alex's brother, Sami, to join us in lighting candles... NJA wasn't the only courageous group, because it took enormous bravery for Sami to come to our event. Jews had just murdered his brother, yet he felt it important to reach out to a Jewish group to say that there was a just resolution of the conflict available to both sides. Also, his fellow Arab-Americans probably suspected him as well for joining with "the enemy." Just as Jews suspected those who embraced Palestinians, the latter suspected their own who embraced Jews. I had enormous respect for Sami's symbolic gesture. After Agenda ran the ad memorializing Alex, I received a

---

59 NJA, "Arab-Jewish Dialogue Influences Nairobi Women's Conference," (Press Release, July 23 1985).
60 Richard Silverstein, "Earl Krugel: Death of an American Jewish Terrorist," *Tikun Olam*, last modified Aug 11 1985 ,http://www.richardsilverstein.com/tikun_olam/2005/11/08/earl-krugel-death-of-an-american-jewish-terrorist/, access date Jan 25, 2012.

threatening phone message on my office answering machine saying (I don't remember everything he said but I'll always remember this phrase): "Odeh was just a fuckin' dead sand n****r. Watch yourselves." I was of two minds about the message. 1985 was still before the age of widespread terror. It was still hard to believe that a Jew would commit murder for a Jewish cause. And in those days (and up to today), the Left deeply mistrusted the FBI. But I resolved in light of Alex's murder that anyone who could leave such a message was capable of causing me great harm. I called an attorney who was a local chapter member and asked his advice regarding what I should do. I then decided to call the FBI. They came to my office (I later got in trouble with the national organization because I allowed the FBI into our office, which we shared with another "controversial" Nicaraguan cultural group), listened to the tape and immediately said: "That's Earl [Krugel,[61] of the JDL]. I'd know that voice anywhere."

This story demonstrates the serious and rabid opposition from right-wing Jewish groups that faced NJA and members of the Arab-American community. This thread of virulent racism and hate from a fringe group within the Jewish and Zionist communities does not represent a widespread position, but it did have the potential for derailing any work towards reconciliation between the Jewish and Arab/Palestinian-American peace movements. To their credit, members of the LA communities were able to continue to work together, despite this violent attempt to destroy their partnership.

Queer Feminism in NJA, and Responding to Homophobia

By 1985, NJA was extremely progressive in its out lesbian and gay leadership and work for lesbian and gay rights in the Jewish community and beyond. That year, NJA published and widely distributed a

---

61   Alex Odeh's murder case is still open with the FBI, over twenty-five years later, and none of the JDL members identified as suspects have been charged or prosecuted. Earl Krugel was jailed on separate terrorism charges in 2001, and was killed by another prisoner in 2005.

groundbreaking pamphlet called "Coming Out/Coming Home" about homophobia and gay rights within the Jewish community.[62]

In April of 1986, the Brooklyn and Manhattan chapters of NJA co-sponsored the first New York community-wide conference on Lesbian and Gay Jews at Stephen Wise Free Synagogue. NJA members including Rabbis Balfour Bricknour, Linda Holtzman, Elly Bulkin, Diana Stein, and Shelly Weiss presented at workshops.

Despite the presence of lesbian and gay Jews, and the leadership of more than a few, there was lingering homophobia within NJA. In her article "A Lesbian Looks at Outreach," Chaia Lehrer wrote of a gay-outreach meeting planned at the home of a homophobic NJA member. Lehrer worried, "What will the well-intentioned but homophobic members of my chapter say in front of these lesbians and gay men we're trying to reach out to? Am I exposing lesbians and gay men to more homophobia?" Lehrer ended up recommending internal education before outreach. The resulting workshop was challenging because a few people were very homophobic, but Lehrer also found it a useful opportunity to express some of the adversity facing lesbian and gay NJA members. She wrote, "Are we expected to pass as straight so that we can 'more effectively address other issues'? Are we welcome in Agenda if we cannot/will not pass? If we come out, can we count on the full support of other members?" Lehrer went on to urge heterosexual NJA members to continue self-education and consciousness-raising, to show up as an ally at gay rights events and find other ways to demonstrate care for gay issues, and to embrace and support the difference of gay and lesbian Jews.[63]

The 1987 National Convention founded an NJA Lesbian, Gay, and Allies Network. It seems that this group was mobilized by anti-homophobia workshops that had been prepared and facilitated by members of the Feminist Task Force throughout 1986 and at the convention.

---

62   NJA, "Coming Out/Coming Home," Pamphlet, 1985.   http://newjewishagenda.files.wordpress.com/2011/11/coming_out_coming_home.pdf

63   Chaia Lehrer, "A Lesbian Looks at Outreach" (*Gesher* Newsletter 1:3, October 1986), 3.

Emergence of the AIDS Crisis

In the 1980s, the HIV/AIDS virus – later to become known as a global pandemic – emerged and began wreaking havoc, with earliest visibility in LGBT communities. Was this a Jewish issue? In March 1986, Avi Rose - a gay man and former national co-chair of NJA - addressed this question in his Co-Chair's Letter in the NJA Newsletter. He reported on a *New York Times* poll from December 18th, 1985 that revealed the range of public attitudes about AIDS, and reported high numbers (over half of respondents) in favor of quarantine, mandatory ID cards, AIDS screening tests for job applicants, closing Gay bars, and tattoos for people with AIDS. Rose writes, "Quarantining people? In camps? With tattoos? Is this a 'Jewish issue?' As Jews and progressive activists, we value compassion, and we value education. If ever there was a need for compassionate, informed response to a crisis, it is now." By this time, Rose was a counselor at the AIDS Project in Los Angeles and in this article he offered reflections on the state of the movement. He wrote,

> Jewish community response has been slow, but it is increasing. Statements have come out from several organizations, and NJA recently participated in a founding meeting of the National Jewish AIDS Project. The community is heading in the right direction, but as usual, needs an extra push. And, as usual, that is a major aspect of Agenda's role.[64]

Though NJA did not work in coalition with major Left-organizing around HIV/AIDS, such as Gay Men's Health Crisis or AIDS Coalition to Unleash Power (ACT UP), HIV/AIDS was on NJA's agenda, especially as an outreach issue within Jewish communities.

NJA's AIDS Working Group (AIDS WG) was founded in July 1986 as a program of the Feminist Task Force. A 1986 update reports that the working group wrote and presented a paper at the National Council meeting explaining what AIDS is, the human rights repercussions, and what Jews could do about it. AIDS WG also contacted the Union of American Hebrew Congregations (UAHC) task force on AIDS and Jewish Family and Children's Service agencies nationally. Finally, the

64   Avi Rose, "Co-Chair's Letter" (NJA Newsletter, March 1986)

October 1986 update reminded readers of the upcoming California vote on the homophobic LaRouche AIDS initiative.[65]

The NJA National Council passed the group's AIDS policy and the AIDS WG presented a workshop on AIDS in the Jewish community at the 1987 National Convention at UCLA, By this time, the National Jewish AIDS Project was already defunct, and Jewish agencies were treating people with AIDS, but not doing any outreach. The working group presenter explained that there was a need to push for both services and visibility. However, in a telling sign of the lack of direction that would face AIDS WG, their statement ended with an acknowledgment that the working group had no strategy at the time, and no financial support was requested.

NJA attended the October 12, 1987 March on Washington for Lesbian and Gay Rights, led by a frontline of people with AIDS (PWAs) in wheelchairs. The march also featured the first showing of the AIDS Quilt at the National Mall. NJA organized a Jewish contingent from their constituency and from outreach to the Reconstructionist Rabbinical College and larger mainstream organizations including the National Council of Jewish Women, National Federation of Temple Sisterhoods, and B'nai Brith. NJA also conducted a Havdalah (end of Sabbath) service for those attending the march.

The day after that historic march, many took part in a civil disobedience action at the Supreme Court regarding the Hardwick decision (which ruled no legal privacy for gay sex) and for civil rights for PWAs. NJA member Avi Rose wrote about his experiences as a gay Jewish man at that civil disobedience protest at the Supreme Court in the January 1988 issue of the Feminist Task Force's Newsletter. Rose's powerful reflection:

> I came there with my affinity group, the Forget-me-nots, which included several of my friends whose lovers have died in the past few years. We had made T-shirts with the likenesses of our lovers and friends, each with his name, and the dates of his birth and death. We had decided to bring their memory and their strength with us onto the Supreme Court steps and into the jails, as part of the

---

65   NJA, "AIDS Workgroup Forms," *Gesher* 1:3, October 1986, 3.

largest act of civil disobedience in Washington since May
Day 1971, the largest ever at the Supreme Court, and the
largest act of Lesbian/Gay CD in history.

And so we did, with a surge of power and vitality that
made a permanent difference for everyone present. We
saw ourselves, in the midst of a plague that decimates
us and an Administration which would be glad to see us
dead, asserting our courage, our wit, and our life/liveli-
ness. (I muse as I list these traits, am I writing now as a
Gay man or as a Jew?)

As over 800 of us got arrested in the course of the day,
many of us participated in yet another ritual of remembrance. People were arrested under the names of Oscar
Wilde, Joan of Arc, Harvey Milk (a modern Jewish hero),
and Sharon Kowalski, a Lesbian severely disabled in an
accident and now locked away in a rural rehabilitation
center, barred from communication with her lover and
community. I was arrested under the name of Magnus
Hirschfeld, a German Jewish doctor referred to as "Gay
Liberation's Zeyde" by Allen Young due to his pioneering
work in Europe in the first third of this century. I wanted
him there with us, too.

In the same article, Rose likened the opportunity to view the AIDS
quilt to a ritual, "an opportunity for remembrance and healing,"
and noted that for many this may have been their first time to really
recognize the gravity of the epidemic or to mourn a loved one whose
funeral was off-limits to the gay community. Rose also wrote that a
friend of his, a Jewish man with AIDS, had come to DC for the march
and had to be hospitalized because of a health crisis. The Intensive
Care Unit where the man spent a week was unaccustomed to treating
PWAs and the healthcare professionals wore ridiculous amounts of
protective clothing. Rose reports that the patient proclaimed that no
one would be allowed into his room with all that gear on, and insisted
on being treated with respect. This was the day before the Civil Disobedience action, and Rose took courage from his friend's resistance.[66]

---

66   Avi Rose, "October in Washington," (*Gesher* Newsletter 2:2, Jan 1988), 1.

By October of 1987, NJA Chapters reported AIDS activism at the local level. The Kadima/Seattle chapter's Feminist Task Force reported work on "education/awareness around AIDS." The newly-formed Louisville, KY chapter reported that they joined with other groups in endorsing a March for Justice sponsored by the Greater Louisville Human Rights Coalition. The March for Justice demands included civil rights regardless of sexual orientation, anti-homophobia education for University of Louisville students, and that "local government units provide funds for a full time AIDS educator." Louisville's NJA had an information table at the rally and distributed copies of "Coming Out, Coming Home," NJA's pamphlet on homophobia in the Jewish community.[67]

Despite the work of a few committed activists within New Jewish Agenda's Feminist Task Force, the organization had little connection with the growing AIDS activist movement. This is especially ironic because organizations like Gay Men's Health Crisis and ACT UP were based, like NJA's national office, in New York City. Jewish AIDS activists of the mid to late 1980's like Larry Kramer, Sarah Schulman, Maxine Wolfe and many others may have been politically similar to the Lesbian and Gay activists of New Jewish Agenda, but there is little to suggest that the organizations collaborated or cross-pollinated in any way. Why wasn't NJA connected to effective organizing around AIDS, activism surely as progressive, political, and crucial as their work around Israel/Palestine or Central America?

In May 1988, Jewish writer and AIDS activist Sarah Schulman wrote, "The progressive community's response to the AIDS crisis has revealed how incapable it is of addressing any issue in which homosexuality is central." Later in the same essay she goes on to explain, "Every week, here in Manhattan, 300-400 people show up at the ACT UP meeting... The room is filled primarily with gay men, then women both straight and lesbian, many of whom work in AIDS-related fields. There are virtually no straight men in ACT UP. I think the overwhelming explanation of their absence is homophobia."[68] But was NJA, an organization with considerable lesbian and gay leadership, disconnected from the growing direct action AIDS movement because of

---

67   NJA, "Chapter Reports," *Gesher* 2:1, October 1987: 5.
68   Sarah Schulman, *My American History: Lesbian and Gay Life During the Reagan/Bush Years*, (New York: Routledge, 1994.)

homophobia within the organization? Perhaps, but it may have been NJA's multi-issue focus and complex democratic process that was a barrier to more effective AIDS activism.

Avi Rose recalled that in his early AIDS activist work, he tried to battle the invisibility of AIDS in the Jewish community by working with family members of AIDS patients, speaking at synagogues with HIV-Positive Jews, and personalizing the issue for Jewish communities. However, by 1985 AIDS activism consumed his political life. It was urgent and couldn't wait for NJA's ultra-democratic process. Rose suggested that the Jewish community's lack of formal involvement in early AIDS activism was not for lack of caring, but for lack of making the connections. "AIDS activism was a singular entity," said Rose, "it wasn't about coalitions and alliances, we were just doing it." Rose was the first full time staff-person working on AIDS in any Jewish community, and is now Executive Director of Jewish Family and Children's Services of the East Bay in California.

New Alliance Party Infiltration

At the October 1987 National Steering Council (NSC) meeting, a member of the NSC identified her/himself as a member of the New Alliance Party and expressed that they had been asked to serve as a connection to the Jewish community for the Lenora Fulani presidential campaign on the NAP ticket. By this time, the national NJA office had already heard from over a half-dozen chapters reporting a sudden influx of new NJA members affiliated with NAP, and invitations from NAP for event co-sponsorships. At that meeting, the NSC discussed relations with the NAP for over four hours.

That December, the NSC passed a contentious resolution about the New Alliance Party (NAP).

> No member of the NSC may participate in a public leadership position in any campaigns, publications or activities of the NAP. Further, the NSC strongly discourages all NJA members from identifying themselves as members of NJA in campaigns, activities and publications of the NAP.

A position paper regarding the resolution briefly explains concerns about the NAP and refers to more information in an attached article:

> A host of frightening disclosures and sobering revelations are made in the accompanying article. They include the relationship between NAP leaders and anti-Semite, neo-fascist Lyndon LaRouche, the manipulative use of psychotherapy to recruit people with emotional problems seeking help to a political agenda, the cult-like and anti-democratic internal operation of the group, the "window dressing" use of women of color to describe the group as Black-led, and the Party's public embrace of Minister Louis Farrakhan whose actual anti-Semitic statements are advertised, published and distributed by the NAP.

The resolution above was passed by a vote of fifteen for, five against, and two abstentions. The NSC also agreed that the staff should distribute information to all chapters explaining what the NAP is and why the resolution was passed. The three-page letter from NJA's Executive Director David Coyne (and attached article by Political Research Associates' Chip Berlet) identified concerns about NAP's apparent attempt to infiltrate NJA, offered some history and context of NAP's dangerous behavior, and also addressed concerns that NJA was "baiting" NAP. Coyne wrote,

> I know that most NJA members and our top elected NJA leaders are extremely scrupulous and determined in their civil libertarian instincts, reflexively and militantly opposed to any baiting or bashing be it "red" (communist/ Communist), "pink (socialist and (C)communist sympathetic), PLO, "terrorist" and gay/lesbian. We have, as individuals and as an organization, found ourselves too often and too recently on the excluded side of just that kind of thinking. This was not an easy discussion for NSC nor was the decision made lightly or without a great deal of concern for both the precedent and the principle.[69]

---

69   David Coyne, "Memorandum re: the New Alliance Party," Dec 18, 1987.

Following the resolution, NJA expelled 20 members of the 21-member Manhattan chapter because of their disruption of the organization and NAP membership. At the July 1988 NSC meeting, notes report that "our confrontation with the infiltration by the NAP evidenced principled political maturity of which we can be proud."

Feminist Task Force Continued

Earlier in 1987, the July National Council meeting passed an amendment requiring two National Council seats to be filled by Lesbian and Gay NJA members. Elly Bulkin and Adrienne Rich, of the Feminist Task Force, were the first two representatives. The NJA Feminist Task Force was a center of powerful organizing and building of political community and shared, deepening political analysis. FTF leaders, recognizing a responsibility to document and spread the word about their work, created *Gesher*, an internal newsletter. *Gesher* included reports from each chapter's FTF and raised feminist issues within NJA.

At the National Task Force meeting in September 1987, the FTF committed to a two-year campaign to discuss issues of family, and began creating dialogue about both traditional and non-traditional families within the Jewish community. On Mother's Day weekend in 1988, the Philadelphia FTF convened a one-day Conference on Women and Poverty at the historic center city Reform synagogue Rodeph Shalom. A *Gesher* article reports that one member of the congregation, on hearing of the conference, responded "Poor Jewish women? I thought they all wore mink coats!" A panel discussion addressed the reality of high poverty rates among all women and discussed how stereotypes of Jewish wealth work to hide the poverty with which many Jewish women struggle.

A few days later, on May 19th 1988, the NYC chapter of the FTF put on a program called "No More Family Secrets: Now We're Talking," co-sponsored with Jewish Women's Resource Center (JWCR), a program of the National Council of Jewish Women (NCJW). Initially, the Jewish Women's Resource Center was hesitant to work with NJA because of Middle East Task Force work (a common barrier to coalition with other Jewish groups). But after three meetings, they agreed to co-sponsor the event. Fliers for the event used powerful statements to get attention and attract people ready for honest conversation. For example, "There are no Jewish battered women," "There are no Jewish alcoholics," and "There are no Jewish incest survivors." The event started with a presentation by Marty Spiegel, and then broke into three groups for discussion: one group for men, and two for women. Of the two women's groups, one was designed for personal sharing and the other for more political (less personal) discussion.

A Tucson FTF program on Jewish Feminism and Social Activism, featuring speaker Adrienne Rich discussed the work of the FTF and the issue of "JAP-baiting."[70] The Tucson FTF also organized a follow-up event on "Eliminating anti-Semitism and Homophobia" co-sponsored with the Tucson Lesbian and Gay Rights Advocacy and Chai Aliz Lesbian and Gay synagogue in Tucson.

The Feminist Task Force Newsletter, *Gesher*, eventually evolved into the beginning of *Bridges: A Journal for Jewish Feminists and our Friends* - a journal that went on to gather and promote a rich collection of voices, powerful analysis, and important writing for another decade after NJA and the FTF ended.

Clare Kinberg wrote,

> In 1988, Jewish writers and editors Ruth Atkin, Elly Bulkin, Adrienne Rich and I started talking about the possibilities of expanding the *Gesher* newsletter into a journal and becoming independent of NJA. Our intention was to be an explicitly Jewish participant in a multiethnic feminist movement; to connect Jewish renewal movements; and to make connections across generations, countries, and languages by publishing archival material and writing in different Jewish languages and in translation.
>
> We wanted to create a forum that would address questions that came up again and again in our writing, organizing, and publishing: Who are Jewish feminists and what are we doing in our own communities? What are our goals? Who are our political allies and how do we

---

70   JAP = Jewish American Princess, a common insulting term referring to Jewish women

discover them? How can others become political allies to us?[71]

The first issue of *Bridges: A Journal for Jewish Feminists* and our Friends launched in 1990. Clare Kinberg served as managing editor until the final issue in Spring 2011.

Debt and Organizational Development

NJA's long-term struggle with debt, at one point reaching at least $60,000, was a major strain on the organization. In October 1987, co-chairs Bria Chakofsky and Marc Gruber described a budget crisis in an internal State of the Organization Report:

> Organizationally, our biggest obstacle is money. Our deficit has increased and lack of funds impact NJA in many ways. National-local relations have been subverted because rebates [on chapter dues] haven't been returned in a timely fashion. Creditors distrust us and cause hassles for our staff. We are understaffed.[72]

Chakofsky and Gruber referred to a tension between NJA National and local chapters due to cashflow issues, but national-local relations may have been a cause as well as an effect of the organization's financial hardship.

In his essay "One Voice Less for the Jewish Left," Ethan D. Bloch, the last chair of the Middle East Task Force, opined that from NJA's founding there was tension between those who wanted to focus energy on building a grassroots movement at the chapter level and those interested in organizing from a strong national center. This strategic dispute led to political disagreements over chapter autonomy and over fundraising issues including "paper members" who paid dues but did not participate in local chapter work. Though paper members were a potential income source, the fundraising strategy was never fully prioritized due to these tensions. Bloch wrote of a combination of political issues that caused a barrier to more effective fundraising:

---

71   in Brettschneider, *The Narrow Bridge*, 30.
72   NJA, "State of the Organization Report", October 1987.

NJA's organizational structure was a compromise between the different camps, and not surprisingly it pleased no one: it was just strong enough so that chapters could not take independent political stances (e.g. on aid to Israel), but not sufficiently focused so that the national could really grow. National leadership, both elected and staff, was never delegated sufficient responsibility, and those responsibilities they did have were never clearly formulated. By default many tasks fell to the two national co-chairs, so much so that many of our most qualified members would not run for these positions.

Activity at the national level can only occur when supported by sufficient paid staff and office resources, and NJA was always understaffed for its ambitions. Money is of course a problem for all radical groups, but NJA seems to have had even more money problems than many comparable groups, due at least in part to the anti-national leanings of some members, to legacies of the 1960's such as a fear of using well-known names (who belonged to our advisory board) in membership drives and the like, and perhaps to a subconscious attempt by younger American Jews to resemble as little as possible the mainstream Jewish life so dominated by fundraising.[73]

In January 1988, meeting notes indicate that the national debt of the organization had more than doubled over the past year from $30,000 to just over $60,000. The organization paid its bills by receiving multiple loans. Treasurer Laurie Kauffman reported that the organization was in better shape than ever but still in trouble. Meeting notes read, "Living with severe debt is horrible and emotionally taxing on the staff and officers. As a result of the precarious state of our finances we can't afford to take risks, can't provide seed money for projects... It is very difficult to plan expenditures when the flow of income is so unpredictable." Chapters struggled to raise money for their local work as well as contributing to the costs of the National organization.[74] Members expressed that staff and Treasurer Laurie Kauffman were

---

73   Ethan D Bloch, "One Voice Less For The Jewish Left: New Jewish Agenda 1981 — 1993," Essay shared with author, May 9, 2008. http://newjewishagenda.files.wordpress.com/2012/01/ethan-bloch.pdf

74   NJA, "Proposed Minutes, NJA National Steering Committee Meeting, Jan 9-11, 1988.

handling the situation extremely well under very difficult circumstances.

The notes also offered insight into more fundraising tensions within the leadership: new NSC members were upset at discovering a financial mess that had to be cleaned up, and expressed frustration about a perceived fundraising competition between the National Convention and a major program: a six-week tour featuring one of South Africa's most prominent rabbis active in the anti-apartheid movement, Ben Isaacson, and a leading Black South African minister, Rev. Zachariah Mokgebo.

U.S. Aid to Israel Debate

Ethan Bloch described another major strategic tension that drained NJA's energy: the issue of opposing U.S. aid to Israel. Bloch described this as the central internal NJA dispute by 1985, one that almost caused an organizational split:

> At the start of the Intifadah in 1987, when media attention to the Palestinian issue could have led to excellent NJA outreach, NJA's Middle East work was paralyzed by the aid debate. A combination of sheer exhaustion, the desire to avoid a split in the organization and changes in leadership, led to a subsiding of the aid debate after the contentious but indecisive NJA National Convention of 1989, dedicated solely to the issue of aid to Israel. NJA's Middle East work never fully recovered.[75]

Before that National Convention, the Middle East Task Force had gathered for a national meeting mediated by George Lakey.[76] There, members agreed to move forward by putting the most controversial issues into discussion through the Internal Discussion Bulletin, NJA's method of handling complicated and lengthy debates. Meanwhile, METF agreed to focus their attentions on lobbying and speaking tours.

---

75 Bloch, "One Voice Less."
76 of Movement for a New Society and Training for Change.

In early 1988, NJA joined in supporting Israeli peace groups' mobilization of progressive representatives at the 31st World Zionist Congress (WZC). In the year before the WZC, NJA collected 650 new members for Americans for Peace in Israel, the US affiliate of Israeli peace group Mapam. Together, NJA, API, Mapam and another Israeli group Ratz (Citizen's Rights and Peace Movement), collected enough votes to bring four delegates to the WZC. NJA METF members Reena Bernards, Gordie Fellman, and Paul Saba attended as supporters. Fellman was to have a seat as a delegate, but the WZC leaders created a new rule about not counting gift memberships, and thereby discredited two of the four Progressive Zionist seats. Still, NJA members were able to use their attendance at the WZC as a networking and movement-building opportunity.

In 1990 and 1991, many U.S. activists' attentions were drawn to the Gulf War. This was the first U.S. war since the founding of NJA, a new challenge both in terms of internal resources and shifting attentions within the larger Left. NJA released a position paper called *The Persian Gulf: Iraq, Israel and the United States* on Sept 7, 1990, before Operation Desert Storm, but they were not able to mobilize a campaign.

Carrying It On Conference

In 1991, the Economic and Social Justice Task Force of NJA organized a major conference: "Carrying It On: Organizing Against Anti-Semitism and Racism for Jewish Activist and College Students" held in Philadelphia Nov 8-10th. Jewish activists and allies (with women making up sixty percent of the attendees) gathered to analyze the relationship between anti-Semitism and racism and to mobilize against institutionalized racism in the U.S.

Julian Bond, African-American SNCC founder, GA Senator, and later chairman of the NAACP, offered a keynote speech detailing the history of black-Jewish relations over the past 250 years in the U.S. Jewish feminist writer and activist Grace Paley also gave a keynote speech about sustaining activism in troubled times. Workshops included Irena Klepfisz's "How Can I Pick Up the Pieces When I Don't Know What/Where They Are? Reclaiming Identity and Undoing Assimulation" and Charlene Mitchell's "Renewing the Dialogue between African Americans and Jews."

Besides a full schedule of workshops, the conference also offered progressive religious rituals led by Philadelphia's Jewish Renewal congregation P'nai Or, and a night of entertainment including storytelling by Grace Paley, music by Rita Falbel, and audience contributions including "fantastical fables, musical adventures, and hot lesbian poems."

The conference received significant criticism, especially for a lack of representation of Jews of Color, reinforcing a false dichotomy between white Jews and African, Latino/a, or Arab peoples. Also, although conference sessions addressing issues of class were well attended and attention was paid to creating a financially accessible conference, participants identified a need for more focus on how class intersects with racism and anti-Semitism. Despite criticisms, conference participants reported leaving the conference feeling inspired, motivated, and re-committed to local organizing around resisting and undoing racism and anti-Semitism.

This was the last official NJA conference.

A Changing World

NJA was losing steam while their long-term campaigns saw major transformations of global politics. In January 1991, the Nicaraguan government signed a peace treaty with guerilla forces, formally ending their twelve-year civil war. In July of that year, the U.S. and the Soviet Union signed the Strategic Arms Reduction Treaty, limiting nuclear weapons proliferation. The Soviet Union dissolved and became the USSR at the end of 1991. In November 1992, Bill Clinton was elected President – the first Democrat in that office since NJA's founding. South African apartheid was formally dismantled between 1990-1993. In September 1993, Prime Minister Yitzhak Rabin and PLO chairman Yasser Arafat shook hands at the White House, and the Oslo Accords were signed. Reflecting on why NJA closed as Middle East peace activism was heading towards the Oslo accords, Gerry Serotta recalled:

"Any real [METF] organizing was way over by Oslo. There was a place in the Jewish community to do that organizing more effectively."[77]

So, Why Did NJA Shut Down?

There is no conclusive agreement about the reasons behind NJA's official disbanding in 1992. A 1993 letter about the closing from National Co-Chairs to chapters celebrates and reflects on NJA's work to foster Jewish organizing, but also notes:

> Paradoxically, this proliferation of progressive Jewish voices was part of the challenge NJA could not overcome. In a more competitive environment, groups with narrower focus and less cumbersome deliberative processes found it easier than NJA to plan programs, attract members and publicity, and raise money.

The co-chairs go on to list, in question form (for example, "Did we have too much Middle East focus or too diffuse a range a concerns?") other issues that may have contributed to the financial crisis and 1992 decision to lay off the paid staff[78] and close the national office. Since the closing, a few other opinions have been published. At the 2002 founding Brit Tzedek v'Shalom conference, veteran Jewish peace activist Cherie Brown reflected on the lessons she had learned over the years, and included these remarks about NJA:

> What did I learn from New Jewish Agenda? That progressive Jews who have functioned in isolation for so long, when given an opportunity to form a national organization with other like minded progressive Jews will find any excuse to recreate the same isolation. It seems just too unbearable to imagine that there is an alternative to functioning on the fringes of the Jewish community.

Brown recalled that leading up to NJA's founding convention, she heard from many progressive Jewish activists who were already strate-

---

77   Serotta added that by 1990, Tom Smerling had started Project Nishma and Johnny Jacoby had started the Israel Policy Forum, and those organizations had merged.

78   Executive Director Irena Klepfisz and Program Administrator Linda Eber

gizing about how to influence the meeting, "already expending energy to set up another fringe caucus." Brown concludes, "What ultimately killed NJA, in my opinion were not only the attacks from the outside, which were many, but also the attacks on each other from within... The staff was never completely trusted or backed to lead the organization. Weakened by ongoing bickering and attacks of each other from within, Agenda finally folded."[79] But Brown's speech does not reflect a consensus opinion from NJA alumni. A year earlier Brown had published the same message in her *Tikkun Magazine* article "Lessons Learned in Organizing American Jews."[80] In response to that article, former national co-chair Christie Balka and former director Reena Bernards wrote a letter to the editor of *Tikkun* arguing that the story of NJA's demise was more complicated. Balka and Bernards offered an overview of multiple issues that, in their opinions, contributed to Agenda's struggles and eventual end.

For instance, Balka and Bernards reflected on the ongoing tensions between NJA's "Jewish Progressive" and "Progressive Jewish" missions:

> At best, it led to strategies that were flexible and creative; at worst it led to chronic disagreements about who we intended to organize and how - perhaps the in-fighting to which Brown refers. Although some of these vigorous debates may have been unnecessary, others were about valid political differences that still exist among progressive Jews.

Balka and Bernards also point to organizational culture as a cumulative issue that contributed to NJA's organizational demise:

> While other national progressive organizations turned their attention away from the grassroots and toward the Beltway, NJA remained committed to grassroots organizing and a vision of participatory democracy. Again, this had both strengths and weaknesses. It engaged many

79 Cherie Brown, "American Jewish Activism; Lessons Learned In Organizing American Jews For Peace In The Middle East," 2002, Brit Tzedek v'Shalom, http://btvshalom.org/conference/founding/brown.shtml
80 Cherie R. Brown, "Lessons Learned in Organizing American Jews," *Tikkun* 16:4, July 2001, http://www.tikkun.org/article.php/jul2001_brown. Included in this volume, Appendix IV.

activists who had previously been excluded from Jewish communal politics, including women, lesbians and gay men, working class Jews, and others, giving us a Jewish and political home. At the same time, NJA's organizational culture demanded a lot of members, decision making was slow, and potential supporters were alienated. NJA's organizational culture resulted in chronic underfunding, and ultimately the organization exhausted its resources.

NJA's organizational culture also reflected the tensions of NJA's "dual focus." NJA members affiliated with Re-Evaluation Counseling brought a focus on group process and identity-based organizing. After 1985, members of NJA's feminist task force often spoke of their goal to build feminist process into all areas of NJA's work. Their influence increased use of "consciousness raising" activist models, and an inward-looking "personal = political" track. Leadership development and commitment to building equitable power dynamics inside the organization were useful strategies, but they were not effective tactics to build the kind of organizing campaigns and solidarity/coalition work that could drive NJA's mission and initial strategy. Many Jewish Leftists, familiar with traditional, mission-driven organizing campaigns, chose not to work with NJA because of the process-heavy organizational culture.

Perhaps because NJA's organizing culture was so process-heavy, its existence supported the development of a number of single-issue organizations during the 1980s. Balka and Bernards explain:

> NJA's radical edge paved the way for other groups to organize a more mainstream constituency. In addition, NJA served as an informal training ground for many who became staff and leaders of these organizations. There came a point in the late 1980s when it appeared that single-issue groups were gaining steam and NJA was not needed as much. If creating a sense of possibility and an infrastructure for progressive Jewish politics is any measure, NJA was surely a victim of its own success.[81]

---

81   Christie Balka and Reena Bernards, Letter, *Tikkun*.16:5, Sept/Oct 2001, http://www.tikkun.org/article.php?story=sep2001_tikkun2. Included in this volume, Appendix V.

NJA's leadership incubation contributed to the creation of many organizations that are viable and active today. As leaders in NJA's five Task Forces became experts in their fields, it may have been advantageous to create single-issue organizations that were not held back by the complicated democratic process of NJA. In other instances, such as that of The Shalom Center, the existence of a single-issue group (working in solidarity with NJA) meant that funding for the project would not be compromised by NJA's controversial politics around Israel or gay rights. NJA's founding as a multi-issue organization had been a strategic attempt to avoid becoming an easy target like Breira, but by the late 1980s the political climate had changed and NJA's multi-issue structure may have been burdensome. Rabbi Gerry Serotta reflected on this trend:

> Jewish feminist groups formed, Jewish sanctuary groups formed, solidarity groups with the Israeli peace movement and all of those things sort of split off from Agenda because it's much easier to do those things than to try to hold together "the movement." But I grew up with the [60's-style holistic] movement so I wanted to start the Jewish progressive movement, not fifteen different Jewish organizations working on [separate] issues. But it's easier to be a Jewish environmental project than it was to hold together a holistic progressive Jewish organization. Since Agenda went out of business, there hasn't been anything like that.

Why did NJA shut down? The answer likely includes all of the above answers as well as the disorientation of a changing international political landscape, exhaustion from right-wing attacks, the drain of the NAP infiltration attempt, and internal dissension on Middle East policy.

Ethan D. Bloch organized the last National Council meeting, which took up the question of whether to fold the organization. He later reflected:

> I have begun to suspect that political organizations have natural life cycles, beyond which there is no point in artificially prolonging life. The changing political world, the

aging of a generation of activists, the failure to organize
the young, the natural decline of organizational energy
as activism becomes routine -- all these led to the natural
dissipation of NJA as an effective political organization
beyond any mistakes we might have made. American
Jewry still needs a grass roots, self-consciously radical
group to nip at the heels of the complacent mainstream
organizations; to promote new ideas that might eventually
work their way to the center; and to be a Jewish voice in
progressive coalitions as the mainstream turns away from
liberal politics. But the issues and organizational styles of
the current decade are not the same as a dozen years ago,
and new groups are needed.[82]

New Jewish Agenda closed shop in 1992, but the lasting impact of
their work is very clear. Two decades later, former NJA members are
found across the leadership and rank-and-file membership of progressive Jewish organizing and cultural institutions, including American
Friends of Peace Now, Jewish Funds for Justice, Jewish Voice for
Peace, J Street, Rabbis for Human Rights, and countless others.

The personal relationships formed in NJA also impacted the course
of individual lives greatly. Many lasting political, creative, and romantic
partnerships evolved from NJA. When I asked former-NJA members
about the group's accomplishments, this was often their first response.

In hindsight, it seems that NJA's work resulted in a series of subtle,
but crucial, cultural shifts that shape our current political possibilities.
For instance, today world leaders talk about a "two-state solution"
in Israel/Palestine as if that phrase has always been acceptable. The
history of New Jewish Agenda (and Breira before that) demonstrates
that advocacy of mutual recognition was once perceived as "suicidal"
for the Jewish community, and Jewish professionals' careers were
destroyed due to their advocacy of the idea. How did this solution
become acceptable in mainstream American and Jewish communities?
The story of New Jewish Agenda sheds light on that shift and many
others.

---

82   Bloch, "One Voice Less."

AUTHOR'S CONCLUSION

When I was just starting to research New Jewish Agenda in 2003, I was hired to organize Jewish youth activists at The Shalom Center, Rabbi Arthur Waskow's Jewish peace organization founded as a spin-off of the Worldwide Nuclear Disarmament Task Force. The Shalom Center aims to mobilize progressive Jews who have been marginalized by the rightward shifts of the largest Jewish institutions. One of my tasks was to strategize about how to reach out to unaffiliated Jews.[83] My first idea was to put up ads and flyers in every Chinese restaurant during Christmas! Realistically, though, I knew that my first task as an organizer was to think with others about the question of *why*: what are the goals and desired outcomes of reaching out to young, unaffiliated progressive Jews? Next, I could look for guidance about how questions: which organizing strategies would help meet the goals my *why* questions identified?

I explored the state of the young Jewish Left by interviewing young (under-30) leaders. My interviewees were activists formally and informally affiliated with organizations including the JEWCY youth-leadership gathering, Jews for Racial and Economic Justice (NYC), Tekiah (Boston), Jews Against the Occupation (NYC), and the documentary film "Young, Jewish and Left."

Filmmaker Irit Reinheimer interviewed fifty progressive young Jews across the US for her documentary "Young, Jewish and Left" with Michael ("Konnie") Chameides. After months of conversations about Jewish identity and activism at the intersections of race, class, gender, country-of-origin, and age, she reported a sense of the current moment that was a strong reflection of the same issues that brought people to NJA. She wrote:

---

83   In the context of Jewish activism, "unaffiliated" is shorthand to describe people who identify marginally as Jewish but don't do anything as Jews or are unaffiliated with Jewish groups or congregations. For example, they may only attend services on high holidays or, in some cases, only "out" their Judaism on the Left when criticizing Israel.

Progressive young Jews lack institutions and organizations that represent or welcome us. For many radical Jews, the organized Left is too secular, straight, and Christian – with either outright anti-Semitism or no room to comfortably practice Jewishness. At the same time, the American Jewish community marginalizes Jews of Color, Queer Jews, and the many Jews who are critical of Israel. Konnie and I both grapple with feelings of alienation from the mainstream Left and Jewish communities. My desire for a loving community that reflects our true experiences as young progressive Jews led me to create this film.[84]

Irit identified the same double-bind that led NJA to work with the mirror-mission "A Jewish Voice Among Progressives and a Progressive Voice in the Jewish Community": Jewish progressives aren't fully "home" in either Jewish or Progressive communities.

April Rosenblum conducted extensive research to write "The Past Didn't Go Anywhere: Making Resistance to Antisemitism Part of All of Our Movements."[85] Through interviews with progressive Jews and allies in the US, Canada, and Argentina, Rosenblum crafted a modern definition of anti-Semitism, and piloted workshops and teaching tools for sharing information with grassroots progressive movements. Rosenblum wrote about why this project was necessary:

There is a new generation of young social justice activists who are realizing how much our Jewishness means to us, and we are reaching for ways to bring who we are as Jews into the activist lives we've built. But many of us are slamming against an unforeseen wall. The more conscious we become of our Jewish identities, the more we can tell that progressive movements have *not* come very far in understanding and resisting anti-Semitism. For us to maintain both our dignity as Jews and our commitments to the causes that matter, we need to speak out,

---

84   Irit Reinheimer and Michael Chameides, producers and editors. *Young, Jewish, and Left.* (2006), DVD. www.youngjewishandleft.org.

85   April Rosenblum, "The Past Didn't Go Anywhere: Making Resistance to Antisemitism Part of All of Our Movements," Pintele Yid. Accessed January 25, 2011. http://thepast.info.

educate our movements, and change the way activists
today respond to anti-Semitism.

April identified a need for analysis and resources that support Jewish
Progressives in the (global) Left. Though NJA did this very work in
the 1980's, the next generation runs into the same "unforeseen wall"
that brought many activists to NJA. For instance, how many activists
of my generation have heard of NJA's crucial analysis-building with allies in the African-American and Arab-American feminist movements
to address the relationship between anti-Semitism and other liberation
movements at the 1985 UN Decade for Women Forum? Must Leftists reinvent the wheel of this analysis in each generation, as some of
us did when the 2001 World Conference Against Racism in Durban
South Africa also devolved into controversy over "Zionism=Racism"
messaging?

And yet, we are not always reinventing the same wheel in the same
context. In the following sections I identify some key shifts in the
post-NJA political landscape: the role of technology in political
organizing, a lack of organizational center for progressive US Jews, a
lack of democracy in national multi-issue Jewish organizations, and a
return to single-issue organizing strategy.

Organizing Offline

Perhaps most obvious in generational changes, technology has completely changed the face and form of activism in the two decades
since NJA shut down. The information age has enabled a shift to
corporate globalization, and global resistance. For instance, HIV/
AIDS, barely acknowledged by government (or Jewish community)
leaders in NJA's time, is now an undeniable global pandemic, and the
AIDS activist community has learned to respond by forging alliances
across cultures and continents to challenge drug company greed and
government neglect.

NJA members struggled to maintain consistent contact through
photocopies, mailings, phone calls, and occasional in-person meetings.
Contentious topics were introduced through Internal Discussion Bul-

letins – collections of research and writing about issues, photocopied and distributed by mail. While I was going through the NJA archives, I often found myself wanting to time-travel and offer the group access to tools such as shared Google documents, track changes, free websites for scheduling meetings or hosting conference calls... even the power of a basic Excel spreadsheet or mail merge would have saved them hours, days, even weeks of work. On the other hand, two of the most measurable outcomes of NJA are the relationships developed within the organization and the leadership development that took place. Would these outcomes have been as powerful in the hyperspeed model of communication that defines our current organizing and mobilizing?

What would New Jewish Agenda have been like if the chapters had been connected through a website, or if online campaigns such as those popularized by MoveOn.org were part of their tactical options? We may be able to guess at this by charting the progress of groups like Jewish Voice for Peace (JVP), which has over 100,000 online members (compared to NJA's 5,000 national membership) and can easily mobilize most of those members to sign campaigns and open letters, and to join together for local organizing campaigns. Many previous NJA members can be found among JVP leadership and membership, but unlike NJA, JVP is a single-issue organization that works for peace in Israel and Palestine with a mission reminiscent of NJA's Middle East Task Force.

No Central Home

As I talked to my peers about current Jewish movement building, I began to understand that despite a rich and deep history of radical Jewish activism in this country, progressive and radical Jewish individuals and local organizations are currently functioning with no central organization that could, like NJA, provide the analysis, support, and resources we often seek.

The mainstream Jewish community builds a unified voice and coordinated strategy through national-level networking institutions like the Conference of Presidents of Major Jewish Organizations, or United Jewish Communities which represents 157 Jewish Federations and

400 independent communities across North America. However, these organizations exclude most radical and progressive Jewish groups from affiliation, as they did in NJA's time.[86] Many Jews are also marginalized by a lack of representational leadership in the biggest Jewish institutions, which have few leaders from among women,[87] out-queers, Mizrahi (Middle Eastern) or Sephardic (Spanish) communities, or other Jews of Color. A phenomenon that some in NJA called "The *Macher*archy," is alive and well in current times.[88]

Since NJA's end, there have been a few attempts to create larger networks for progressive American Jewish activism, but none has made the radical choices that defined NJA as a multi-issue membership organization committed to work against international, internal, and structural oppression. The first major post-NJA attempt to network local social justice groups came in Fall of 2000, when a dozen regional groups gathered to create the Jewish Social Justice Network (JSJN), a "forward-looking *chutzpahdik* [gutsy] movement" which aimed to network organizations, not individuals. By Fall 2003, that network had closed due to loss of funding.

In Spring 2005, the Jewish Council on Urban Affairs in Chicago convened a conference of Jewish organizations active in urban justice work—meaning local and national, not global justice issues.[89] That conference, *Tzedek Yalin Bah: Justice Shall Dwell There*, brought together over 250 people from seventy-five organizations across the U.S. The conference was an opportunity for movement building and comparing best-practices, but it did not result in an ongoing central network until 2009, when the Nathan Cummings Foundation founded and funded the Jewish Social Justice Roundtable (JSJR), convening a network of eighteen local-activism Jewish groups. JSJR's most visible work as of this writing has been shared creation of mainstream service-learning

---

86   In the 1980s, there was a gathering of the "Conference of Presidents of Minor Jewish organizations," an idea I'd love to see revisited (Brettschneider, Marla. Cornerstones of Peace. 155 N151)

87   See Jewish Women Watching for creative exposure of this issue www.jewishwomenwatching.org, also Ma'ayan's 2003 Report "Listening to Her Voice." http://www.jccmanhattan.org/category.aspx?catid=1013

88   *Macher:*"big shot" or, more specifically "a man with contacts" (Yiddish).

89   Reportback online at http://www.shalomctr.org/files/JCUAreportback.pdf I attended this conference, and organized a spontaneous workshop for intergenerational dialogue about the history and impact of New Jewish Agenda, when I realized that nobody was acknowledging NJA's history and the lessons that could be applied to the work of the conference. Many NJA alumni were in attendance at the conference.

opportunities and a day-long meeting with the White House in Summer of 2011 to discuss domestic policies and priorities.

Lack of Democracy

While the initiative to create more space for overlapping activism between local Jewish social justice organizations is an admirable one, and the work of moving mainstream Jewish conversations towards social justice is always an incremental process, when I compare the trajectory of JSJR with that of New Jewish Agenda, the differences are – to be honest – heartbreaking. JSJR's story, from founding to present, starkly reflects the general trend of the non-profitization of movement building. While JSJR represents a network of (now twenty-one) local membership-based organizations, there is little hope for the rank-and-file of those movements to build power together without the controlled translation of their national leadership, who are the only people in the decision-making rooms. And what happened to the seventy-five groups that gathered for the 2005 conference? Surely fifty-four local activist groups didn't disappear over a five-year span, so why such a small subset of the original gathering? Meanwhile, JSJR seems to be funded exclusively by a single (Family) Foundation, not a membership base or other grassroots fundraising method – an indication of JSJR's lack of accountability to its members, or even member-organizations. Another sign that JSJR is anything but a grassroots national network is the surprising reality that as of this printing (at least two years into JSJR's development) the Roundtable doesn't even have a website or any way to be directly contacted. In fact, the most informative public document I could find was a Craigslist ad for an Executive Director search.[90] The following quote by Jon Rosenberg, JSJR Member and CEO of Repair the World, sums up the limitations – the reinforcing of the "macherarchy"- of JSJR's model. In a 2010 interview with *The Jewish Daily Forward*, Rosenberg reflected that:

> Within an ecosystem of organizations that have overlapping but distinct missions, and with a concept as challenging as social justice, it's unrealistic to expect that a platform and a distinct set of activities will emerge

---

90   Craigslist.org. PostingID: 2732304968. Accessed Dec 2, 2011.

quickly. In my view, one of the most important things that has come out of the Roundtable is the forging of social capital, the ability to pick up the phone and speak to people I now know personally.[91]

Compare this model of a "newly emerging coalition of Jewish social justice organizations working together to establish a unified and powerful Jewish social justice movement" with the founding process of New Jewish Agenda. In NJA, a small group of local Jewish activists wrote a "New Jewish Manifesto" in December of 1978 and within two years, through a transparent public process, they had coalesced hundreds of activists representing groups across the country to a founding convention that created a platform and distinct set of activities within a short time. In NJA, this happened without already-committed funding and without sacrificing the necessity of activism around international issues, including Israel/Palestine. Why was this model of democratic grassroots movement-building a possibility in the 1980's but not now? This change reflects a trend toward professionalization of movement-building over the past three decades, away from radically democratic member-leadership for systemic change and towards a paternalistic model of "repairing the world" through service.

Multiple Agendas

The most defining feature of New Jewish Agenda, compared to organizations before or after them, is their history of simultaneously organizing an explicitly Jewish voice in local, national, and international justice movements. Their work for justice and peace in the Middle East (especially Israel/Palestine), Central America, and South Africa (opposing Apartheid) was hand-in-hand with their work for social and economic justice in their own backyards. This kind of intersectional connecting-the-dots between local and global movements is nowhere to be found in our current Jewish activist landscape. As another NJA researcher, Joanne Lehrer, explained in 1995 : "The late 80s and 90s saw a split between the Israel-focused and American-focused radi-

---

91   Jo Ellen Green Kaiser, "The Roundtable' Is Offered A Seat: Social Justice Groups To Have Strong Presence at G.A." *The Jewish Daily Forward*. August 13, 2010. http://www.forward.com/articles/129833/

cal Jewish movements, which had come together for almost two decades."[92]

The current scarcity of intersectional Jewish organizing is due to this political and cultural reality: *Jewish groups active on domestic justice issues* (such as U.S. poverty or LGBT rights) *are pressured to maintain a neutral position on the issue of Israel in order to find allies within both the Jewish community and diverse grassroots movements in the US.* Today, political questions about Israel are posed so often to Jewish groups doing domestic organizing that we commonly refer to these questions as "the litmus test." In my experience, domestic organizing groups tend to take subtle positions that attempt to balance the grief and blame between Jewish/Israeli and Palestinian communities – hoping that a one-time statement will make the questions go away without anybody yelling too much or derailing the campaign work altogether.

I'm frustrated by the lack of global-local analysis in my Jewish activist communities, but it's hard to place blame when I recognize that we must build within a fracturing political climate in which Jewish groups critical of Israel function at a disadvantage, marginalized in the Jewish community and unable to build coalition on other issues affecting Jews. Meanwhile progressive Jewish groups focused on any issue besides Israel must maintain a neutral or explicitly pro-Palestine position on Israel/Palestine and all other Middle East politics in order to build bridges in Left coalitions. And there's more to the complicated story:

- Often Jewish domestic-issue groups are unable to join coalitions that make connections between local, national, and international issues for fear of implied position on Israel. For example, Jewish organizations working to counter anti-Arab and Muslim discrimination after 9/11 were sharply criticized and sanctioned by larger Jewish institutions because they allied with Arab and Muslim groups perceived as anti-Israel.

- The majority of progressive Jewish activists are not explicitly part of the *Jewish* Left. While they might be raised Jewish (culturally Jewish, or religiously obser-

92   Joanne Lehrer. *Jews, Justice and Community: An Analysis of Radical Jewish-Identified Organizing in the United States.* 1880-1995. Division III Thesis. Hampshire College, 1995: 71.

vant), that identity might not be a core part of their work on, say, environmental justice. Jewish progressives most often publicly mention their Jewishness in relationship to their position on Israel, as in "I'm a Jew against the Occupation." This contributes to a lack of visibility for many Jews among the diverse progressive movements in the US.

- For Jewish Leftists, identifying ourselves publicly can be a loaded choice even if Middle East issues are not on the table. Classic tropes of anti-Semitism accuse Jews of being nefariously *over*-represented in (and controlling of) Communism, Socialism, Anarchism, Union organizing, and the Left in general. That anti-Semites also accuse Jews of controlling the world through international Capitalism is an irony lost on most conspiracy theorists.

As a result, we currently see a proliferation of single-issue Jewish progressive organizations, including many with vastly overlapping subject areas and constituencies, and only subtle differences in positions and strategies. These similar organizations are in competition for funding and places at larger tables, often leading to tense or hostile relationships with each other, weakening the potential of the movement in general.

Nu? A New New Jewish Agenda?

So, is it time for a *New* New Jewish Agenda? This research begs the question, "Should we do it again?" The answer is: Yes and No. *Yes*, the progressive Jewish community would benefit from a central organizing effort that applies feminist process and values, uses multiple campaigns to address the interconnectedness of oppression, fights anti-Semitism and racism, values queer visions of family, and operates through democratic decision-making without dependence on charismatic and controlling leadership. And *No*, the NJA model would not be appropriate today.

NJA was primarily formed by the first generation of American Jews that really had to choose whether to assimilate. Their parents and grandparents (some of whom also joined NJA) grew up in an America that saw Jews as off-white, as dirty immigrants and Communists. The generation who built NJA were reclaiming Jewish identity in both a secular Left and an assimilating Jewish community.

My generation follows that era's successes and failures, and as a result we have a different task. We have only known a political landscape that includes *intifada*. We have been invited to love Israel as a Jewish state by the Birthright program but we have rarely been shown why Judaism is so precious. We have seen the devastating effects of nationalistic movements, and we have only been offered more nationalism as protection. We have seen identity politics implode when too simplistically applied, but we have also seen the power of intersectional politics that value our overlapping identities. We've seen a wide diversity of Jewishness and we've also witnessed the argument about who gets to speak for "the Jews" played out over and over, ad nauseum.

We do need a *new* "New Jewish Agenda," and while the shape of our organizing may be very different today, the issues we face are closely intertwined with the story of New Jewish Agenda. Like those in NJA, we must build relevant Jewish culture in a progressive political context. We must demand feminist and anti-racist transformation of ourselves and our organizations. We must push for the transparency and accountability of grassroots organizing and direct democracy. We must be courageous in our critique of Israel but also refuse to raise our Jewish voices *only* in critique of Israel. We still need to build political power by choosing winnable campaigns and not simply battling over the hazy target of public opinion. We still need to honor and heal the very real fears of targeting and annihilation that motivate our communities. And we also must be clear in our ethical motivations and not allow our community's work to be based solely in fear. We have to have the guts and honesty to connect-the-dots between local and global politics.

But our tactics have to change to suit our current political times. The trend of Social Forums at the global, national, and local levels and other emerging global justice gatherings point towards collaboration and networking to build unity and strength around common goals, while building insight and analysis about the growing edges and conflicts within our struggles. The new Occupy Judaism movement, and the Occupy movement as a whole, have reinvigorated strategies of mass mobilization and direct action that challenge the trend of professionalization of social change work, and bring new voices from the margin to the people's mic every day.

As I write, we're witnessing the beginning of a new global justice movement, and we can't yet know exactly where our most powerful opportunities will emerge. What we can know, can study and learn from, is where we've been and how the last few wheels got invented and re-invented - and what we want to carry with us or leave behind from those stories. The history of New Jewish Agenda is one of a popular movement that modeled intersectional analysis, that lifted marginalized voices, that addressed internalized oppression with creativity and even some humor. It's also a story of a movement that faced infiltration, debt, serious debate over core mission issues, and the problem of how long it takes to really practice democracy. Sound familiar? These are challenges that activists wrestle with every day throughout our movements. Let's study this history, talk about it together, and dig even deeper into the roots of our political work today. For as the sage Hillel once asked, "If not now, when?"[93] And as another Jewish sage, Adrienne Rich, added: "If not with others, how?"[94]

---

93 Pirkei Avot 1:14
94 Adrienne Rich, "Reflections on Being a Jewish Progressive in 1985," Speech to NJA National Convention, 1985. http://www.theshalomcenter.org/content/reflections-being-jewish-progressive-1985

ACRONYM LIST

ACT UP: AIDS Coalition to Unleash Power

ADC: Arab American Anti-Discrimination Committee

AFSC: American Friends Service Committee

AFSI: Americans for a Safe Israel

AIDS WG: AIDS Working Group of the Feminist Taskforce

API: Americans for a Progressive Israel

CAJE: Conference on Alternatives in Jewish Education

CJF: Council of Jewish Federations

DSA: Democratic Socialists of America

EC: NJA Executive Committee

FTF: Feminist Taskforce

IDF: Israeli Defense Force

JDL: Jewish Defense League

JFREJ: Jews for Racial and Economic Justice

JSJR: Jewish Social Justice Roundtable

JWRC: Jewish Women's Resource Center

JVP: Jewish Voice for Peace

METF: Middle East Task Force

NAACP: National Assoc for the Advancement of Colored People

NAP: New Alliance Party

NCCJ: National Conference of Christians and Jews

NCJW: National Council of Jewish Women

NFTY: National Federation of Temple Youth (Reform Judaism's youth group)

NGO: Non-governmental Organization

NJA: New Jewish Agenda (also referred to as "Agenda")

NSC: NJA National Steering Committee

OCNJA: Organizing Committee for a New Jewish Agenda

PJA: Progressive Jewish Alliance

PLO: Palestinian Liberation Organization

PWA: Person/People with AIDS

RC: Re-Evaluation Counseling, or Co-Counseling

SNCC: Student Nonviolent Coordinating Committee

UAHC: Union of American Hebrew Congregations

WANJA: Washington DC area chapter

WZC: World Zionist Congress

AFTERWORDS

There is an Alternative:
Historical Storytelling & Political Practice
Rachel Mattson

"I believe in history. Jewishness is not… a religious identity, it's not a national identity, it's not an ethnic identity,
it's not a cultural identity, it's not a racial identity, it's not
a philosophical identity, it's not a dietary identity, it's not
a theological identity. More than anything, the only thing
that, for me, can truly encompass Jewishness, is that it's a
historical identity. Which means there is something about
what Jewish has meant in the history of people who have
identified themselves as Jews, that somebody identifies
with."

-Daniel Kahn[1]

What you're holding in your hand is without a doubt the most comprehensive published study of the 1980s-era radical left Jewish organization, New Jewish Agenda (NJA), in existence. Although NJA was a
pivotal organization, one that offered a bridge between the 1970s-era
of radical social movements and the small and slow rebuilding era
of the 1990s and 2000s, information about its strategy, its campaign
work, its rise and its fall has been, until now, generally hard to find.
Indeed, until Ezra Nepon created a website devoted to exploring the
history of the organization (in 2007), information about NJA existed
mostly in the rawest archival form. The next most comprehensive
publicly available "account" of the group seems to be the Online
Archive of California's digital finding aid for the records of the Los
Angeles Chapter of New Jewish Agenda (1979-1991).[2] After that, you

---

1   Sarah Anne Minkin, "Daniel Kahn on A Tradition of Subversion and a Subversive Tradition," Jvoices.com, March 27, 2009.
2   http://www.oac.cdlib.org/findaid/ark:/13030/ft4h4nb0t3/

might also be able to locate a couple of unpublished graduate theses on the subject. But that's pretty much it.

It's maybe not a coincidence that it took person like Nepon —an independent scholar— and an organization like Thread Makes Blanket —an independent press— to publish this sort of study. I don't want to overstate the case, but the truth is that in the traditional spaces of American intellectual life - universities, university presses, scholarly journals - debate about Jewish politics and history is constrained. Rabidly pro-Israel organizations like Campus Watch closely monitor campus speech, threatening, intimidating, and, at times, attempting to blacklist any university professor who, for instance, effectively criticizes Israel's policies toward Palestinians.[3] And though it is not often openly discussed, scholars wishing to study the history of anti-occupation organizing in the U.S. —even, or especially, among Jews— know they must prepare themselves for a firestorm of scrutiny, critique, and possibly, politically calculated rejection by those who might help them with their work. That's on the one hand.

On the other hand, historians of Jewish America have generally been preoccupied with three overarching topical questions, none of which demand inquiry into the how and why of a short-lived, 1980s-era, lefty Jewish group. Broadly speaking, studies of Jewish American history have tended to explore the following questions: a)What factors explain the migration of Jews to North America?; b)How did Jewish immigrants "become" American?; and c)What accounts for the rise and fall of Jewish American liberalism in the 20th century? From Irving Howe's classic *World of Our Fathers: The Journey of the East European Jews to America and the Life They Found and Made*[4] to *Michael Rogin's Blackface, White Noise: Jewish Immigrants in the Hollywood Melting Pot*,[5] the history of Jewish America has been rendered, most effectively, as a series of struggles by immigrants and their offspring to contend with American geography and culture. For certain, these questions have provoked, and continue to provoke, some wonderfully creative, surprising, and important studies - including Josh Kun's recent account of the 1940s-era "Jewish-Latin craze" (a movement shaped, in part, by a generation

---

3   On the chilling effect of the work of organizations like Campus Watch's see, for instance, Michael North, "We Have Our Eye on You… So Watch Out", *Times Higher Education,* January 28, 2005.

4   Simon and Schuster, 1976

5   University of North Carolina Press, 1998

of young Jews seeking to reimagine their Jewish American experience by dancing to music by bands with names like Juan Calle and his Latin Lantzmen, and recordings bearing titles like "Mazel Tov Mis Amigos"[6]).

Still, this literature fails to sufficiently explore or explain —among other things— the deep roots, and the broad contours, of political and social conflict among Jewish Americans. Studies like Susan Glenn's *Daughters of the Shtetl: Life and Labor in the Immigrant Generation*[7] tell of intergenerational cultural conflict, illuminating something of the ruptures that occurred within immigrant families as younger generations began to express themselves as *Americans*. But intergenerational family conflicts were not, by a long shot, the only sorts of rifts that have marked the history of Jewish communities in the U.S. Political conflicts, the historian Michael Staub (author of *Torn at the Roots: The Crisis of Jewish Liberalism in Postwar America*[8]) argues, also go back a very long time, and run very deep. But because questions about these divisions remain on the sidelines of Jewish American historiography, we have (to quote Staub) "no sense of just how embattled" Jewish American leftists have historically been. Likewise, we fail to appreciate just how "energetically and creatively" right-wing Jews have put forth "antileft and antiliberal arguments."[9] And here the two hands come together: we have no understanding of how energetically right wing elements have historically attacked the left; and because progressive historians continue to face their creative attacks, it is difficult to find support for studies that attempt to trace the contours of these attacks.

Ezra Nepon's *Justice, Justice Shall You Pursue: A History of New Jewish Agenda* —and the website that was its precursor— builds outward from studies like Staub's, deepening our understanding of debate and division within Jewish communities in the 20th century US. Offering an alternative history of the 1980s, and a glimpse at post-1967 oppositional Jewish politics and practice, this study helps us envision the possibilities that are held within both the past and the future. As Nepon herself puts it: "I developed this project because I needed to hear these stories" - in order to enlarge her imagination of what's possible.

6   Josh Kun, "Bagels, Bongos and Yiddishe Mambos, or The Other History of Jews in America" *Shofar: An Interdisciplinary Journal of Jewish Studies* 23(4) 2005

7   Cornell University Press, 1991

8   Columbia University Press, 2002

9   Staub, p. 6

"I have a hunger for this information," she recently told me. "It's my own family story, basically."

You might notice, as you read the manuscript, that the organizing framework —and the central questions at issue— don't fit neatly into the concerns that prevail within Jewish Studies, as described above. Although *Justice, Justice Shall You Pursue* does shed light on the histories of Jewish American "liberalism" and Jewish American identities, in the end, it is not primarily concerned with either. Instead, Nepon tackles a set of distinct questions about the nature of Jewish activisms in the late 20th century. How did radical Jews respond to the politically conservative climate of the 1980s U.S.?, she asks. What has queer and feminist Jewish organizing looked like, historically? What might re-examining and remembering histories of late 20th century Jewish radicalism offer to Jewish activists working to make change today? These are questions that, while unfamiliar and perhaps discomfiting to many professional historians of Jewish America, make a great deal of sense to anyone who has spent time in the trenches of Jewish activism and cultural work over the past two, or three, or four decades. Lots of us have struggled to invent new ways to be Jewish, and to make new kinds of Jewish community and culture - wrestling, as we went, to align our Jewish identities and our activist desires.[10] Along the way, we searched for stories about our historical peers. Rumors we had plenty. But narrative, detailed, critical accounts were hard to find — and precious. *Justice, Justice Shall You Pursue* doesn't promise to unlock the mystery of Jewish activisms; it doesn't give easy answers about how to work towards international and domestic justice. But it offers a starting point for the sorts of conversations that will help us deepen our own answers to the dilemmas of doing solidarity work, engaging in collective action, and making Jewish radical culture.

If you don't know your history, you are doomed to repeat it is one sentence that I'd prefer to never encounter again. I think if I ever met one of, say, Etgar Keret's wishes-granting goldfish, this would be the first wish

---

10   And here I just have to give a shout out to the late great Adrienne Cooper, who died way too young in 2011 and who contributed enormously to the project of reclaiming radical Jewish traditions from a slightly different direction. For a primer on Adrienne's enormously important work, see, for instance, Joseph Berger, "Adrienne Cooper, Yiddish Singer, Dies at 65" *New York Times,* December 28, 2011.

I'd wish for.[11] I would especially wish to never again hear anyone using this idea to explain why they think history is *important*. I'll ignore, for the moment, the fact that the idea that *history repeats itself* a mindless, boring, wrong cliché, and focus instead on this: this phrase suggests something disturbing about the purpose of education and historical study. Is historical inquiry, then, simply a tactical practice? And if so, shall we only study episodes in the past that offer clear "lessons" for us in the present? In short, must we only examine the past in order to avoid repeating the mistakes of our historical counterparts?

In my view, no. In my view, historical study is useful for a lot of very different reasons, reasons that have to do with the human imagination and the development of a critical lens through which to view the contemporary world. On one hand, there's the point made so eloquently by the cultural critic C. Carr in 1992: "Dissent," she wrote, "cannot happen in a vacuum." Tangible alternatives - in the form of stories about the past, and communities we create in the present - make up "the fabric that sustains experiment, stimulating that leap into the void and maybe even cushioning a fall."[12] Then there's the point that Adam Green and Charles Payne, historians who study African American protest movements, have made: historical stories offer up critical ingredients that help us "envision alternative futures and the steps that lead there."[13]

And there are other points, including one which was most astutely rendered by Michel Foucault in the various studies to which he devoted his life: that learning about the past reminds us, among other things, that the world we live in is not the inevitable result of some pre-destined chain of events; that instead we live in the wake of the struggles that our predecessors waged.

Justice Justice Shall You Pursue suits all of these purposes, and nicely.

Take, for instance, the case of *tikkun olam* - the Hebrew phrase most commonly translated as *repair the world*. If you've spent time anywhere near the non-orthodox Jewish communal or non-profit worlds, you

---

11   Etgar Keret, "What of this Goldfish Would You Wish?" in *Suddenly, a Knock on the Door: Stories* (Farrar, Straus and Giroux, 2012)

12   C. Carr, "The Bohemian Diaspora," *The Village Voice,* February 4, 1992

13   Adam Green and Charles Payne, eds., *Time Longer than Rope: A Century of African American Activism, 1850-1950* (NYU Press, 2003), p. 5

will have heard this term. Although "once regarded as the property of the left," to quote Rabbi and public intellectual Jill Jacobs, "the term is now widely used by mainstream groups such as synagogues, camps, schools, and federations, as well as by more rightwing groups."[14] It has been embraced, she observes, by Jews of various political and religious persuasions - as well as by non-Jews (including Bill Clinton and Cornel West) seeking to align themselves with Jewish values and communities. And it has been deployed to describe, and justify, a wide range of (often conflicting) activities - from "teaching Torah" to "volunteering for social service agencies," "raising money for Israel" to "supporting the creation of a Palestinian state."

If you attempt to discover, as I recently did, the origins of this now nearly ubiquitous phrase, you will undergo a short course in Jewish philosophy. Jacobs - who has done a thorough study of this topic through the lens of religious history - explains that the phrase initially came to life in the 3rd century. It appears in ten separate places in the Mishnah - "the first attempt to codify Jewish oral law" (handed down in the 3rd century) - mostly, notably "in relation to problems in traditional divorce law." This, however, is not the *tikkun olam* with which we are so familiar now. In the Mishnah, "tikkun olam" was used to describe those actions undertaken specifically *to fix a flaw in law or custom* that would otherwise undermine the coherence of smooth flowing of society. So for instance: although it was technically legal for a man to send his wife notice that he was divorcing her and then change his mind without notifying her, such actions in practice threatened to undermine the family and social order - and so, in the spirit of *tikkun olam*, they were officially outlawed.

Jacobs notes that the phrase makes a brief appearance in the Aleynu prayer (likewise developed in the 3rd century) but again, here its meaning is quite unlike the meaning ascribed to it in the Jewish communal world today. Thereupon it fell into disuse, reappearing only in the sixteenth-century, when a Kabbalist Rabbi named Issac Luria used the phrase to suggest that following halakhic law and performing mitzvoth could have a positive effect beyond one's own life - could literally, even, heal the broken shards of the cosmos. (Jacobs, 2007; Wolf, 2001; Breger, 2010.) The history gets thin from there on out. After the 16th century, Jacobs notes, the term largely disappeared

14   Jill Jacobs, "The History of Tikkun Olam," *Zeek*, June 2007.

from popular usage. Until the mid-to-late-20th century. In the 1980s, she explains, "liberals and leftists" started using it, giving it new life. But what exactly happened in the 1980s? How did *tikkun olam* gain its new life, and new connotations? Here Jacobs' account - as well as most other accounts of the term's history - peters out.

Justice, Justice Shall You Pursue offers evidence that begins to fill in that historical gap. Indeed, evidence contained herein suggests that the founding members of Agenda deserve a great deal of the credit for wrenching an idea that had been a strictly mystical, almost magical notion about the relationship between human action and the natural world, from the depths of the Mishnah and the Kabbalah into the everyday vernacular of Jewish social action. Take a peek, for starters, at the founding document of New Jewish Agenda - the 1979 "Call To Action" letter. "Dear Friends," the letter begins.

> Over a period of years, some of us have thought, studied and acted together in a variety of contexts and organiza-tions. We have grappled with issues and questions such as the following: How can we democratize the American Jewish community? How can we create a Jewish culture relevant to our own needs and time?...How can we con-vince American Jewry that its longterm survival may well be linked to support of progressive causes outside of the Jewish community?[15]

"We believe that the time is now," the letter continues, "to declare our criticism of the false dichotomy between 'Jewish' issues and other concerns" by creating a new union of progressive Jews. The letter concludes: "We believe strongly that authentic Jewishness can only be complete with serious and consistent attention to *Tikun Olam* (the just ordering of the physical world and human relationships)" and "we believe it is time to join together" to bring this about.

There it is. *Tikun Olam.*

Was this the very first late-20th century instance in which the idea of *tikun olam* was used as a call to organize against political and social injustice? I can't say for sure. But if it wasn't the very first, it was

15   See the full document in this volume, Appendix I

certainly a very important, very early articulation of this now-familiar idea. I haven't yet seen any earlier document from the 20th century that uses *tikkun olam* in this way.

In order to understand this document (and its importance in the modern historical journey of *tikkun olam* and NJA), it is helpful bear in mind, as Nepon explains in the body of her text, that in the decade just prior to the writing of this 1979 call to action, the conservative wing of the American Jewish community had decimated, through vicious attacks, several progressive Jewish organizations, including the D.C.-based multi-issue group Jews for Urban Justice, and the national call for Middle East peace, Breira. In assaulting the work of progressive Jewish organizations, right wing leaders of the 1960s and 1970s had used a tactic that many 21st century Jewish activists will find familiar: they critiqued both the political analysis of leftist leaders *and* their legitimacy as Jews. One critic argued, for instance, that progressive Jewish activism was a manifestation "of Jewish self-hate, an illness afflicting our people too long"; another wrote that there was "no place" for leftists "in the American Jewish community."[16]

As they planned to launch a new progressive union of Jews in the wake of these events, then, it seems the founders of New Jewish Agenda deliberately framed their work within a distinctly Jewish frame. Perhaps they did this in an effort to gather ammunition against anticipated attacks on their right to speak as Jews. In any case, they found and repurposed a Hebrew phrase, with roots in ancient Jewish mysticism and philosophy. Reclaiming the Lurianic idea of *tikkun olam* within a secular framework, NJAers were bolstering their belief that acting against racism, international human rights abuses, and military aggression were legitimate Jewish practices.

It is hard, from this far away, to appreciate just how creative a move this was. Don't forget: when this call to action was written, *tikkun olam* was not in regular circulation in the Jewish communal or secular worlds; it was not a yet a cliché. Indeed, neither its transliteration nor its translation were yet standardized: here it is "tikun" (with one k) instead of "tikkun" olam, and "the just ordering of the physical world and human relationships," instead of "repair of the world." The fact that the authors of this manifesto neither spelled nor translated the

16   Staub, pp. 159; 202; 293.

phrase in the way to which we are accustomed today might not be hugely significant in the long run, but these facts serve to remind us just how fresh their use of the phrase was. In using *tikun olam* to describe their Jewish beliefs, these young activists were trying out a new idea, based on their interpretations of Jewish texts and contemporary Jewish life. In this way, NJAers were reinventing Jewishness, and crafting a fresh and relevant sort of Jewish identity—one that made sense in their context of their lives, their historical moment, and the specific stresses they faced as young disapora Jews in the 1970s/80s U.S.

Within a decade, of course, more and more Jews would begin to use the idea of *tikkun olam* to describe Jewishly oriented activism. By 1987, members of NJA were themselves routinely using the term in their literature - now, with the standardized spelling (two k's) and a new translation (somewhere between 1979 and 1987, the translation featuring "repair" had taken root). And, as we know, in the 30 years that have elapsed since, the phrase has been adopted by a wide set of institutions and individuals. Today, it is commonly called a "core Jewish value" - even by middle of the road Jewish institutions.[17] But the meaning and resonance of the term has mutated. Michael Lerner, founder of the liberal *Tikkun* magazine, has criticized the ease with which Jewish organizations have adopted "the language of *tikkun olam* without its substance."[18] Lerner has a point. The way that most Jewish institutions use the phrase these days bears little resemblance to the concept that NJAers forged in the late 20th century. No longer framed as a call to mobilize against economic injustice, global warfare, or international atrocities, *tikkun olam*, here, requires only that we as individuals volunteer occasionally to paint public buildings or clean up a park. Disappointing as it might be that the original, radical meaning of tikun olam has been watered down, it is worth remembering that even the presence of this watered down idea of social action as a core Jewish value wasn't the inevitable result of centuries of Jewish practice. It was an idea drawn from Jewish tradition that a group of visionary Jewish activists struggled to make relevant in a new era.

17   See, for instance, a recent report commissioned by the Charles and Lynn Schusterman Family Foundation, "Jewish Service Learning: What is and What Could Be: A Summary of an Analysis of the Jewish Service Learning Landscape," written by Ellen Irie and Jill Blair (BTW Consultants, Inc.), May 2008, p. 1.
18   Lerner quoted in Marissa Brostoff, "Beyond Repair," *Tablet,* September 3, 2010.

Understanding NJA's role in shaping history and meaning of *tikkun olam* performs the valuable task of making the contemporary world strange to us. It reminds us that the world we live in isn't the inevitable result of an inevitable series of events; it was, on the contrary, caused by a set of struggles, compromises, victories and defeats. It suggests that Jewishness is not a static category - that, in fact, what even mainstream institutions consider to be "core Jewish values" can change, or at least mutate, and that collective action has effects beyond the immediately imaginable. It reminds us that the world we live in - and the shape of contemporary political and cultural conflict - was created out of the muck of struggle and conflict. It reminds us that we live in the wake of the struggles that our predecessors waged. And it reminds us that our actions in the present might have value beyond what we can glimpse right now.

Maybe the idea *if you don't know your past you're doomed to repeat it* sounds so hollow to me because I have a hunch the past is full of possibility, full of events and ideas we might actually *want* to repeat.

———————————

As I began planning and sketching out my ideas for this essay, I found myself struggling more mightily than usual to maintain a veneer of professional disinterestedness. I found myself wrangling - again, even more than I usually do when I write about the past - with a range of strong emotions. On one hand, this is because Ezra Nepon is a personal friend. A personal friend who has, over the half-decade I've known her, enlarged my world in ways that I'm not sure I've ever really articulated. Its not just that she's a clear thinker, a delightful performer, and a smart political strategist. Its that she manifests her political and personal desires in the most inspiringly *look out world, here I come* way. I'm not really sure how she does it, but she's able to see possibilities in corners of the world that look to me like desolate and scorched earth. Nepon is, for me, a critical element of the fabric that sustains my experiments; she is someone whose stories have, for a long time now helped me envision alternative futures and the steps that lead there.

Indeed, Nepon's very ability to articulate her desire for a history of NJA falls into this category. Even though my own life was, in some deep way, changed by my brief brush with Agenda, it never occurred to me that I needed an account of New Jewish Agenda to help me sustain and envision alternative presents and futures.

In 1991, when I was a very young, very naïve undergraduate at Oberlin College, I attended NJA's final conference, "Carrying It On: Organizing Against Anti-Semitism and Racism for Jewish Activist and College Students." Having been raised in the milquetoasty mush of suburban American reform Judaism, I was new to activism, new to anything but the most bland, reform Jewishness, new to a lot of the things that would, ultimately, grow to give my adult life purpose. At Oberlin, I'd joined up with a small anti-Zionist Jewish campus organization, composed of activists who were not as new as I was to radical politics or complex Jewish culture. One of them found out about the upcoming NJA conference, and told the rest of us about it - and before I knew it, I was piled into a car, driving overnight to Philadelphia to participate in this gathering. What happened, then, was this: my 21-year-old mind blew apart. I sat in a ballroom, and heard Julian Bond and Grace Paley give heart-churning speeches. I met Jewish activists of all ages. I attended break-out groups. I signed petitions and mailing lists. Its just impossible to explain, now, the effect this gathering had on my political and aesthetic imagination. I'd come from the absolute middle of the road; my parents had never attended a protest or a rally in their lives, there wasn't a labor activist or a blacklisted Communist in our entire lineage. This conference, and the people I met there, showed me something different - familiar, deeply familiar. But also very different from what I'd been raised to imagine. It was there that I really connected with several people who went on to found the NYC-based Jews for Racial and Economic Justice (JFREJ). Within two years, I was working at JFREJ; in the many years that have elapsed since then, that organization has continued to be, for me, an important activist home.

Until I read Nepon's study of NJA, I hadn't really understood what I was brushing up against in Philadelphia in 1991. In the years that followed, I'd heard stories about NJA. But I never really got a clear picture of what the organization was, who and what created it, what kinds of battles its members had waged, or any number of other, related questions. Nor could I place my own life in relationship to the historical events of which Agenda was a part. I did understand the power that Agenda had; in some ways, the possibilities of my own life had been expanded by that power. But without this study, I might never have known much more about Agenda than that. More important, maybe, is that without this study I wouldn't have appreciated the ways in which Agenda served to educate the imagination of a generation. Not just me - but many, many others.

In his study of 'zines and radical culture in the 1980s and 1990s, cultural historian Stephen Duncombe suggests that the political uses of alternative community and stories, though seemingly hard to pin down, are actually quite tangible. "The powers that be," he writes, "do not sustain their legitimacy by convincing people that the current system is The Answer. That fiction would be too difficult to sustain in the face of so much evidence to the contrary. What they must do, and what they have done very effectively, is convince the mass of people that *there is no alternative*." Zines, alternative communities, and other kinds of countercultural work, he argues, offer the idea that there are, in fact, many alternatives.[19] This is, in a very clear way, what radical Jewish organizing has offered dissatisfied American Jews for decades - in some cases quite *literally*. Indeed, it was the right's insistence that there was no alternative to Israel's military aggression against Palestinians and Arabs that gave rise to one of Agenda's immediate predecessors: the very important, short-lived, Jewish peace organization Breira: A Project of Concern in Diaspora-Israel Relations (1973-1978). As Nepon puts it, "The name, Hebrew for 'Alternative,' was a response to the common phrase '*Ain breira*' or 'There is no alternative' - an Israeli Labor Party slogan used to justify military aggression much in the way 'National Security' is used in American political rhetoric."[20]

Justice, Justice Shall You Pursue invites readers to imagine alternatives of various kinds. Alternative pasts, alternative presents, alternative futures. Alternative ways of collecting together. Alternative approaches to inquiring into the past. Alternative methods of publish books. Alternative methods of dissent. Alternatives to the idea that *there is no alternative*.

---

19   Stephen Duncombe, *Notes from Underground: Zines and the Politics of Alternative Culture* (Verso, 1997), p.10
20   This volume, p..10

If we are, as Daniel Kahn so eloquently observed in the epigraph to this essay, a people that are brought together and brought about through historical stories, then it matters a great deal what sorts of stories we tell, what sorts of stories we cultivate and hold close to our hearts. *There is something about what Jewish has meant in the history of people who have identified themselves as Jews, that somebody identifies with.* There are lots of stories still to be told about radical Jewish pasts, and we're not telling them fast, or imaginatively, enough. Meanwhile, lots of people and powerful institutions marshal support for a different story about what Jewish means, and what histories matter to the Jewish past—stories which, all too often seem designed to foreclose our imaginings of what it has meant, and what it could mean, to be a Jew in diaspora. This book offers activists - especially young queer Jewish activists - stories that can help make sense of the political worlds we live in, and the ones we might inhabit in the future. Narrating several of the many ways that radical Jewish organizing has been vulnerable and fragile and precious, it reminds us of the possibilities of Jewish activist work, how to be a decent human, and how to make the world a more just place. It reminds us of the need for careful attention and study and always, always action, despite the trouble we might face down the road.

(Works Cited on p. 146)

Rachel Mattson is a historian, a writer, an educator, and an occasional puppeteer. She works as an Assistant Professor at SUNY New Paltz, where she teaches courses in U.S. history, memory and performance, critical pedagogies, and gender and sexuality. She is the author of numerous publications including "Theater of the Assessed: Drama-Based Pedagogies in the History Classroom" (Radical History Review 2008) and History as Art, Art as History: Contemporary Art and Social Studies Education (Routledge 2009, cowritten with Dipti Desai and Jessica Hamlin). She is a member of the Aftselokhis Ladies Auxiliary Home for the Aged, a political performance and archival collective, and serves on the boards of the Pop-Up Museum of Queer History and Circus Amok, as well as on the faculty advisory committee for Jewish Voice for Peace's We Divest campaign.

Hidden Agenda: Lessons from NJA, Lost and Learned

Daniel Rozsa Lang/Levitsky

In the decades since New Jewish Agenda shut down, its ghost has been a constant presence in Jewish radical organizing, but rarely an openly acknowledged one. To the extent that young Jewish radicals hear about Agenda at all, it is generally in the form of a cautionary tale whose message varies according to the storyteller's political orientation.

> Remember Agenda? You can't mix local work with Palestine solidarity. Remember Agenda? You can't have a mission that combines economic and racial justice with feminism and queer liberation. Remember Agenda? You can't create a national multi-issue organization with actual radical politics. Remember Agenda? You can't have both democratic, anti-hierarchical structures and effective organizing. Remember Agenda?

But the answer to the rhetorical question, really, is no. We don't remember Agenda. We weren't part of it. Many of us were too young to have known it existed. And until recently, no one has been particularly interested in making it possible for us to connect to those memories, that history. This project, in its online form and now this paper one, is the first real attempt to share Agenda's story with younger cohorts of Jewish radicals and to think about what its history can mean. The fact that it's only happening now, nearly two decades after Agenda shut down, is a shonde, a bushe, and a kherpe - a shame, an embarrassment, and a disgrace.[1]

For the wave of Jewish radicals I belong to, and the ones that have followed us, this silence where our recent history should be has been

---

1   In the over-the-top Yiddish call-out phrase preferred by Steve Quester - a queer Jewish radical active in ACT UP/New York, Jews Against the Occupation/NYC, and the United Federation of Teachers, among other things.

both a gift and a theft. In some ways we've lacked the grounding that we could have gained by hearing about the movement work that shaped many of our mentors and friends. Reading the draft version of this book, for instance, was the first time I heard about the place of Agenda in my dear friend and comrade Rachel Mattson's Jewish radical life. On the other hand, not knowing this history has helped us to feel free to build our own approaches and models for what Jewish radicalism can be, and to create structures to put them into practice. The results have been organizations like Jews Against the Occupation/NYC and the Aftselokhes Ladies Auxiliary Spectacle Committee; films and plays like *Young, Jewish and Left, An Olive on the Seder Plate,* and *Between Two Worlds (who loved you before you were mine?)*; bands like the Shondes, Yiddish Princess, and Schmekel; research and analysis projects like *The Past Didn't Go Anywhere* and this very book. I'm writing this today as a result of that freedom: my friendships and comradeships with Ezra Nepon, Rachel Mattson, and Abigail Miller are all rooted in this ferment of Jewish radical projects, in particular the purimshpiln that Jews For Racial and Economic Justice and the Aftselokhes Spectacle Committee have created for the last decade.[2] This is a world, however, in which even where there are Agenda veterans present, the silence around Agenda has persisted.

Part of our older comrades' reluctance to talk about Agenda has to do, I believe, with a sense of shame about the organization's end, and a feeling that it was a failure because it is no longer active. To me, the opposite is true. A progressive organization with a decade-long lifespan is a success, and one that maintains dozens of chapters and a membership of thousands, with multiple areas of active work, even more so. And still more successful is one that gives itself a clear ending, rather than clinging to a paper existence and preventing its members from fully moving on to other projects. Agenda's decision to declare an end rather than trailing off into ambiguity is one that more organizations should make. That insistence on honesty and clarity is the very thing that can make moving forward through other organizations and structures an act of strength, not the retreat that some Agenda veterans seem to have felt it to be.

---

2   A project initiated by Yiddish singer and scholar Adrienne Cooper (of the Workmen's Circle/Arbeter-Ring) and driven forward by theatrical genius Jenny Romaine (of Great Small Works).

But what happens when we do listen to this organizational ghost? The range and unpredictability of the possible answers to that question are why I'm so excited about this project - and in particular the paper version, which can pass from hand to hand in a different way from its online incarnation. I'm eager to see what the folks I've organized with over the past fifteen years, and the folks who've come up since then, do with this history, these memories.

To me, some of the most important things we gain by paying attention to Agenda have to do with the lasting tensions and longstanding questions within Jewish radical organizing. These are structuring elements of our work that we share with the members of Agenda, but about which we have lacked the angle of vision and analysis that comes from their experience. Sometimes, the history of Jewish radicalism since Agenda can clarify things then left hazy; sometimes the reverse; and sometimes the combination can bring to light what neither experience makes visible on its own. Here are a few of the areas where I see insights emerging from the re-connection of Agenda to our collective memory.

> *"What is the point of having a separate*
> *Jewish organization?"*
> (I.F. Stone, at the NJA founding conference)[3]

As Allan Solomonow writes, introducing Stone's query, this is "the question others refuse to ask", which "disturbed many" at the gathering that founded Agenda. It is still a question which raises hackles and elicits trite and unconvincing answers from Jewish progressive organizations. For the most part, we hear many versions of the "light unto the nations" myth of Jewish moral superiority, sometimes in the guise of pseudo-history ('we the greatest victims of the 20th century' or 'we the most radical of U.S. immigrant groups'), sometimes in theological clothing (usually somehow involving the recently devised link between 'tikkun olam' and social justice)[4]. Even if these types of

---

3   As cited in Allan Solomonow, "A New Agenda for American Jews", available at http://newjewishagenda.files.wordpress.com/2011/11/new-agenda-for-american-jews.pdf
4   For which, as Rachel Mattson points out, Agenda itself likely deserves much of the credit. This innovation is itself one of the most fascinating re-writings of religious tradition around, transforming the Lurianic kabala's reincarnation-based explanation for some people's greater inherent holiness into a cornerstone of contemporary Jewish liberation theology. Most accounts of the term's roots, like Jill Jacobs' otherwise thorough article for *Zeek* [available at http://www.

answer involved less rhetorical acrobatics and more historical accuracy, they would still contain all the problems of any racialized essentialism. More persuasive answers are to be found, however, in Agenda's history, especially in aspects of the group's practice which have carried through into more recent projects. I'll talk here mainly from my experiences as an active member of Jews For Racial and Economic Justice (JFREJ) and Jews Against the Occupation/NYC (JAtO).

A first answer is strategic: the mobilization of privilege. In its participation in the Central American solidarity movement during the 1980s, Agenda made effective use of the moral authority U.S. Jews were seen to have around refugee issues and questions of political asylum. It also took advantage of some of its members' access to Jewish religious institutions to spur synagogues to participate in the Sanctuary movement. JFREJ has used this strategic approach more explicitly and constantly, in a range of ways: using access to affluent congregations to organize progressive employers of domestic workers in support of the Domestic Workers Bill of Rights legislation; taking advantage of racist overvaluing of Jewish voices on Muslim and Arab issues to fight anti-Arab racism in the New York City Department of Education; etc. In ways that many other projects cannot, specifically Jewish groups can find strategic resources in both the unjust social privileging of Jewish voices in certain contexts and in the concrete privilege - economic, racial, etc. - of certain parts of Jewish communities.

This approach can, of course, turn toxic. When it erases poor and working-class Jews to focus only on the wealthiest, echoing the racist stereotypes of the *Protocols of the Elders of Zion*, for instance. Or when it does not explicitly challenge the anti-Arab racism and Islamophobia that privileges Jewish voices over those of Palestinians, Iraqis, Iranians, Pakistanis, Egyptians, etc., or endorses Jewish gatekeeping over those communities' public political presence. Examples of these particular failures, and other similar ones, aren't hard to think of among liberal and progressive Jewish organizations. The challenge of mobilizing privilege lies exactly there: in figuring out how to fight the

zeek.net/706tohu/], deliberately avoid detailed examination of 'tikkun olam''s radically anti-egalitarian Lurianic history, despite its recent proponents' explicit grounding in that kabalistic tradition and the versions of its deep conservatism that surface in their 'spiritual progressive' politics.

structures that create it while exploiting it for tactical advantage - and in seeing when that's not possible and the strategy should be avoided.

A second answer is cultural and affective: "creating a political home", as the NJA 1987 draft mission statement put it. Or, to phrase it more specifically, establishing a space based on political affinity in which social ties and cultural connections can create and feed a genuine community of struggle. A shared point of identification beyond political positions - even Jewishness, with all its various meanings and versions - seems to help that process, defining a space in which we can move more easily between strategy and pleasure, ideology and intimacy. The kaleidoscopic, creative, exuberant, emotionally charged tone I hear in descriptions of Agenda's founding convention and street actions sounds delightfully like my experiences in JFREJ and JAtO - the sign of a live community excited to be raising hell together. Both of those projects have explicitly understood their strength as coming from the strength of the personal relationships and collective feeling they create. I see that as a hallmark of Agenda's legacy, if not an explicit part of its approach, and as an experiential answer to Stone's question.[5]

This, too, can have its failures and toxic forms. For instance, when a shared Jewish identity is in fact a shared white and Ashkenazi heritage, or a shared upbringing in 'mainstream' suburban observance, or a shared middle- and upper-class background. Or when 'Jewish identity' itself is used as a synonym for Zionist political commitment or religious belief. Or, more simply if more subtly, when shared cultural reference points and resources become an essentialist politics of identity, reproducing the myth of Chosen superiority and forming a barrier to strong alliances with other radicals and social movements. Again, examples aren't hard to find. And again, the fact of failures marks the importance of this answer as well as its complications.

---

5   This is, of course, not a dynamic original to Agenda. Radical movements have always succeeded or failed based on their ability to create living cultures of struggle and communities of resistance, radical Jewish projects no less than others. The Bund, the sizable Jewish component of the U.S. Communist movement (within the Yiddish section of the International Workers Order and beyond it), the Workmen's Circle/Arbeter-Ring and other institutions of the Jewish labor movement – all thrived in large part because of their roles as the organizational anchors of a creative, vibrant culture and community. And from the first Bundist pamphlet in the form of a Hagaddah, printed in 1898, to the past decade of JFREJ-sponsored radical Purimshpils, Jewish radicals have taken full advantage of the cultural resources of our communities to create that culture. Agenda, as the first multi-issue organization to do so on a national scale in the U.S. since the Red Scare, takes its place in that tradition.

These two answers together articulate not just an explanation of "what is the point" of specifically Jewish radical projects, but an analysis of the areas where such projects can be more or less useful in different organizing contexts. They ask us to look concretely at the position of our particular Jewish communities and think about where there are resources of material or social privilege to be tapped, where there are cultural resources that can help draw us together. The results of that inquiry will look vastly different in the Persian Jewish neighborhoods of Los Angeles, the suburban Ashkenazi world of Newton, MA, the longstanding Syrian Jewish enclave of central Brooklyn, the often-overlooked Jewish community of Eugene, OR. In some places, the important task may be creating a home from which Jewish radicals can participate in work outside specifically Jewish projects; in others creating a structure to connect Jewish community resources to an ongoing struggle; in still others, addressing the particular needs of a Jewish community facing attack. And in each case, the necessary close attention to the internal diversity of the community will, in practice, disrupt these simple descriptions. The framework that makes all of these routes visible as possible paths for a Jewish radical group is, however, one that grows from these two answers to Stone's question, as seen in Agenda's history and practice and in the experience of projects descended directly or indirectly from it.

> *"...parliamentary jabberwocky... balloons and scaffolding on their heads...*
> *The Dead Caucus..."*
>
> (Jonathan Mark, on the NJA founding conference)[6]

The most visible aspect of Agenda's dozen years of activity, to those of us who didn't experience the organization directly, has been its end, and in particular the debate over its causes. Most of the time, arguments about the cause of Agenda's shut-down seem to center on identifying one or more defining tensions within the organization. Sometimes the argument is that the wrong position prevailed – as, for instance, in Cherie Brown's insistence that the absence of "one key leader who will be in charge" was at the heart of the organization's problems.[7] More often, writers present tensions more neutrally, with

6   In "Toward a New Jewish Agenda: The Left's Last Chance", as cited by E. Nepon at http://newjewishagenda.wordpress.com/njas-story/founding-convention-december-1980/
7   In her talk at the founding conference of Brit Tzedek v'Shalom, available at http://btvshalom.org/conference/founding/brown.shtml

the implication being either that the resolution necessary to bridge the contending positions was not found or that no resolution was possible. The tensions identified in various analyses are likewise varied: centralization vs. localism, attention to process vs. program positions, democracy vs. hierarchy, and, perhaps most frequently, a focus on Agenda's role as "a Jewish voice among progressives" vs. "a progressive voice among Jews".

To me, the most striking thing about these arguments is the fact that they almost invariably present these tensions as logistical, as aspects of the organization's mechanics and infrastructure. Only very rarely are they acknowledged as the *political* tensions they are. Christie Balka and Reena Bernards, for instance, in their rebuttal to Cherie Brown, group "commit[ment] to grassroots organizing. . . participatory democracy. . . . engag[ing those] excluded from Jewish communal politics. . . [slow, non-hierarchical processes for] decision making" and approaches to fundraising as problems of "organizational culture"[8], leaving little if any room to understand each of these as an active political choice. This example is particularly significant because the political issues involved are central to Agenda's work, self-understanding, and legacy: democratization of the Jewish community and of the U.S.; feminism and queer liberation; a class analysis of Jewish communities and the U.S. more generally; attention to the economic side of political influence and power.

This urge to create a depoliticized understanding of Agenda's internal tensions and eventual end comes in large part, I believe, from a desire to disconnect these elements of Agenda's politics from the one issue that is – constantly – acknowledged as a political tension involved in the organization's demise: Palestine.

Whether directly, as in Ethan Bloch's essay "One Voice Less for the Jewish Left"[9], or indirectly, as in Balka and Bernards' piece (glossed as "valid political differences that still exist among progressive Jews"), political differences between Zionists and non-Zionists,[10] in particu-

---

8 In "Why NJA Disbanded", available at http://newjewishagenda.wordpress.com/njas-story/why-did-nja-shut-down/why-did-nja-disbanded/

9 Available at http://newjewishagenda.files.wordpress.com/2012/01/ethan-bloch.pdf

10 Those actively opposed to Zionism were not welcome in Agenda. The founding conference's resolution on Israel (that framing itself marking off a limited range of possible positions) begins "We are committed to the State of Israel" and goes on to make "Jewish national self-

lar around U.S. aid to Israel, are almost always cited as a factor in Agenda's end. But whether mentioned explicitly or not, questions related to Palestine and Zionism are always kept carefully separated from other aspects of Agenda's politics and organizational structure. Bloch, for instance, devotes the entire "Political Problems - External & Internal" section of his analysis to Palestine, while everything else is grouped together as "Organizational Problems". This pattern has been followed in the structure of most if not all Jewish progressive and radical organizations founded since.[11] California's Progressive Jewish Alliance, for instance, explicitly places its positions on "Peace and Dialogue: Israel" outside its "primary task [of] working to create a just and equitable society."[12] Similarly, JFREJ was in its 12th year when it adopted an anti-Occupation position - and that was made possible in part by its inclusion in an anti-war statement made in 2002, when the U.S. war on Afghanistan made it impossible for the organization to continue to take positions only on issues local to New York City. The experience of Agenda is often held up as a justification of this isolation of political questions around Palestine and Zionism from all other issues.

The supposed lesson from Agenda here is twofold. It proposes, first of all, that separating out the question of Palestine will protect Jewish progressive and radical organizations from attack by the Jewish right, and provide legitimacy within Jewish communities. Secondly, it promises that this strict division between Palestine-related organizing and all other work will make it possible to escape conflicts inside Jewish radical and progressive projects. In practice, however, neither of these has proven true.

---

determination within the State of Israel" the key criterion of Agenda's support for peace efforts. [cited in Lewis Moroze, "New Jewish Agenda - A Welcome Voice", available at http://newjewishagenda.files.wordpress.com/2011/11/nja-a-welcome-voice.pdf] Similarly, the very first words of the 1982 Agenda flier "Some Examples of Our Work" are "From the point of view of our commitment to Israel and deep concern for its survival and well-being". [Available at http://newjewishagenda.files.wordpress.com/2011/11/some1982actions.pdf]

11   Aside, that is, from those specifically focused on Palestine solidarity work. Groups doing work related to Israeli policy which use a 'peace' or 'dialogue' framing rather than one centered on 'justice' or 'solidarity', however, generally do follow this standard post-Agenda path. The Tikkun Community is typical, if particularly overt, in its "Core Vision" statement, which removes "Peace, Justice and Reconciliation for Israel and Palestine" from "Struggles for Social Justice and Peace" into a 'special case' category of its own. [see http://www.tikkun.org/nextgen/tikkuns-core-vision]

12   Progressive Jewish Alliance web page "About: Peace & Dialogue: Israel", available at http://www.pjalliance.org/article.aspx?ID=18&CID=3

In relation to other parts of the Jewish community, the record is very clear. The Progressive Jewish Alliance did face deeply destructive attacks during its first years from within the Los Angeles Jewish community. But not because of its stance on Palestine - because it targeted the sweatshop working conditions at Guess?, owned by the Marciano brothers, whose wealth brings them notable influence within the Jewish institutions of Southern California. JFREJ, on the other hand, was consistently targeted as "anti-Israel" long before it adopted any position on the Occupation. Neither of these experiences is unique, or particularly unusual, for Jewish progressive and radical projects of the past two decades. And neither JFREJ or PJA - the flagship progressive groups in the country's largest centers of Jewish population - has achieved the level of recognition by 'mainstream' Jewish community institutions that Agenda itself achieved - holding membership in the Jewish Federation Council of Los Angeles, for example, as well as proposing and passing resolutions in the General Assembly of the Council of Jewish Federations.

The question of internal conflict is harder to measure. I can only speak with full confidence about JFREJ, where I've found a political home since 1999 as both a rank-and-filer and Board member. For JFREJ, neither a decade of explicitly declining to take any position on anything related to Palestine nor a decade of holding a basic anti-Occupation position and explicitly not taking on concrete work directly related to Palestine has prevented drama around Palestine and Zionism. What I've heard over the years from comrades and friends in other organizations suggests that this experience is typical, whether or not a group has taken a specific political stance on Palestine, and regardless of what that stance is.

But the fact that this 'lesson from Agenda' is quite simply disproven by actual experience doesn't mean that these tensions - in Agenda and in more recent projects - aren't related to the sustainability of Jewish radical organizations. It does, however, invite us to look directly at how these acknowledged political tensions around Palestine and Zionism connect to the tensions within Agenda (and other projects) that are presented as if they were not in fact political. And through that examination, to see what's there is to learn when we set aside this false lesson.

"[T]hose who seek an end to our oppression because they recognize
that an injury to one must be the concern of all"
(Carol Haddad)[13]

The aspects of Agenda's "organizational culture" which Balka and
Bernards single out as sources of tension are a useful place to start.
They center on questions of democracy within the organization and
within the Jewish community more generally, echoing the announce-
ment of the organization's founding conference and the conference's
resolutions, which called for an end to "elitist and non-responsive"
community leadership, and for active efforts towards full participation
and leadership by those excluded from the macherarchy: "working-
class Jews, women, the young and elderly, poor, disabled, single and
single-parents, geographically isolated, gay and Lesbian Jews and
recent Jewish immigrants."[14] This is the set of issues that directly
connected Agenda's core politics to its home communities. These are
the struggles in which the organization brought to bear on the Jewish
world its commitment to racial and economic justice, to feminism and
queer liberation, and to participatory democracy rather than hierarchical structures. The firm political decisions Agenda made here,
refusing to apply a different standard to its internal processes and to
the Jewish community institutions it dealt with than it did to 'outside'
forces, are one of the strongest elements of its legacy.

But this political consistency is what becomes invisible when these
positions are presented as logistical or organizational questions and
depoliticized. It is precisely what the question of Palestine is carefully
removed from, both in accounts of Agenda and in other organizations' current practice. If we look directly at it, we can understand
the tensions within Agenda quite differently, as deeply entangled with
the direct contradiction between the group's positions on Palestine
and the consistent politics of the rest of its work. In some areas this
is quite overt, involving directly conflicting positions on U.S. government policy as well as contradicting Agenda's overall anti-racist and
anti-militarist politics. For example, Agenda condemned both U.S.
and Israeli military aid to Central American regimes fighting dirty wars

---

13   In a letter to NJA Executive Director Reena Bernard, on behalf of the Feminist Arab-
American Network, available at http://newjewishagenda.wordpress.com/?attachment_id=174
14   As cited in Lewis Moroze, "New Jewish Agenda - A Welcome Voice", available at http://
newjewishagenda.files.wordpress.com/2011/11/nja-a-welcome-voice.pdf

against popular movements and indigenous peoples, while remaining unable to take a clear position on the U.S. military aid that supported Israel's nearly identical actions.

In other areas the dynamic is more subtle, and ties more directly into the questions of hierarchy and exclusion. In an exchange of letters between Agenda and the Feminist Arab-American Network concerning a meeting called by Agenda about "the conflict"[15] leading up to the 1985 UN Decade for Women conference in Nairobi, Carol Haddad pointed out the ways in which the meeting's structure - including an exclusively Jewish planning group, a restrictive agenda, extremely short notice, and other problematic elements - ran directly against the organization's overall politics, especially around exactly these issues of democracy and process. More generally as well, Agenda members were well aware - and frequently pointed out - that the most visible anti-democratic actions by U.S. Jewish institutions are those directed at both Jewish and non-Jewish critics of Zionism. The presence of this critique, however, does not makes the organization's otherwise broad struggle for greater community democracy harmonize with its own similarly-structured core principle of "commitment to Israel".[16]

In current organizations we see the same pattern, perhaps most noticeably in connection with anti-racist work. While U.S. Jewish communities are now generally unwilling to tolerate overt racism against African Americans and increasingly reluctant to frame prejudice against latin@s in racial terms rather than xenophobic ones, explicitly racialized hostility towards Arab Americans is if anything on the rise, fed by the Jewish right's organizing and media campaigns on behalf of the Israeli government. Groups like JFREJ and PJA, which consider anti-racist work in Jewish communities to be part of their core mission(unlike Palestine-related activity), consistently find themselves

15   A phrase apparently left without further specification in Agenda's invitation (critically quoted in the letter by Carol Haddad cited above), inviting the question of how Agenda did in fact define the question of Palestine: as a Jewish/Arab ethno-racial conflict? a Jewish/Muslim religious one? an Israeli/Palestinian nationalist one? an Israel/Egypt/Jordan/Syria international one? a settler/indigenous colonial one?

16   In this case, there is a particular irony, given the importance of Jewish institutions' successful attacks on the (Zionist) peace group Breira to the founding of Agenda. Similarly, JFREJ was founded in large part as a response to the 'mainstream' Jewish community's efforts to shun and discredit Nelson Mandela after his release from prison because of his support for Palestinian liberation. The clear, consistent politics of anti-racism and anti-colonialism of this founding moment lends a (rather depressing) irony to later tensions within the organization around Palestine and Zionism.

faced with attacks on Arab individuals, institutions and communities that are specifically about Palestine. They've managed to respond vigorously and effectively to specific cases, including the attacks on Debbie Almontaser and the Khalil Gibran International Academy in New York, which began with racialized red-baiting about the word "intifada". None of these organizations, however, seem to have been able to make the leap to broader, more active organizing against anti-Arab racism within Jewish communities. In the case of JFREJ, at least, there has in fact been a sharp decline in the organization's anti-racism workshop program since the beginning of the Al-Aqsa Intifada in 2000, when directly addressing Palestine while talking about anti-Arab racism became impossible to avoid.[17]

Similar, if more subtle, tensions are visible around community democracy and organizational structure. No current Jewish radical group I know of includes the democratization of Jewish community institutions in its political agenda, and few even go so far as to directly challenge these institutions' right-wing politics. JFREJ, for instance, did picket a New York City Jewish Community Relations Council meeting over its refusal to condemn the police murder of Gidone Busch in 1999, but did not apply even that degree of pressure as part of its organizing around the similar killings of non-Jewish men, and has not focused organization energy on the JCRC as such. This is in part an acknowledgment of the minimal role that the 'major' Jewish institutions actually play in the lives of most U.S. Jews, but it also evades the task of taking seriously – and challenging – their role as the supposed sole legitimate representatives of Jewish communities in this country. It is, now as in Agenda's time, in relation to Palestine and Zionism that these institutions are most visibly unrepresentative of U.S. Jews' actual beliefs, and most actively hostile to the very notions of democratic decision-making and open political discussion. And the inseparability of their anti-democratic structures and their Zionism, I believe, is why they have not been confronted by Jewish radical organizations willing to insist on democracy in workplaces, education systems, and urban planning processes.

---

17 One aspect of this is reduced interest in these workshops as overt anti-Arab racism has become more acceptable in more Jewish contexts, but the frequency of trainings for trainers and other work that makes these programs possible also trailed off quickly in the early 2000s.

Alongside this, there has been a distinct retreat from horizontal organizational structures. While radical and progressive movements over the last decade have generally have moved more and more towards non-hierarchical models, whether centered on consensus processes or other models for participatory decision-making, Jewish progressive organizations have moved in the opposite direction. At the 2005 national conference on Judaism and social justice hosted by Chicago's Jewish Council on Urban Affairs, for instance, in two days of programming attended by 250 progressive and radical Jews representing 75 organizations there were no workshops dealing with questions of internal democracy or decision-making. And while the conference's round table discussion by the Executive Directors of the best-funded organizations present was interrupted with a structural critique of this kind, the intervention was made by another Executive Director. On the organizational level, JFREJ is fairly typical in that this retreat has been framed as a shift towards a 'community organizing' model, which just happens to centralize decision-making in staff and (largely staff-anointed) key 'volunteers'[18] The result is less space for direct contact, discussion, and argument among rank-and-file members, sharply reducing the possibilities for thinking politically about the work of the organization as a whole and assessing its basic political consistency. And, along the way, making it far more difficult for rank-and-filers to even see how to affect the organization's direction or positions, especially on issues like Palestine which are already separated off as 'too controversial' or 'not what we work on'. As it was in Agenda, this is a political problem rather than a logistical one – do we believe strongly enough in the critiques we make of the structures of the world around us to actually build alternatives to them?

The Agenda experience, I believe, shows the actual stakes for Jewish progressive and radical organizations in how we address the political questions around Palestine and Zionism, and the particular dangers in the model for addressing them that Agenda pioneered and that other groups have since followed. The story of New Jewish Agenda makes it very clear that separating questions around Palestine and Zionism off from the rest of an organization's politics and treating them as

---

18   These models, largely drawn from the Alinsky tradition's explicitly hierarchical rather than participatory approach, are also heavily funded and promoted by liberal foundations and philanthropists. A key marker of this shift in many contexts is a shift in referring to those who participate in an organization's work as 'volunteers' rather than 'members'.

a 'special case' - whether or not doing so leads to actively disruptive conflicts within an organization - can undermine a group's ability to maintain the consistent commitment to justice that makes radical work coherent and effective. This dynamic is particularly visible in Agenda's history precisely because the organization was so effective in nearly all other areas at linking the politics it expressed in its internal structure and its public work, and because so many of its victories seem to grow directly from that political coherence.

At present, as we strategize the growth and evolution of current Jewish progressive and radical projects, we have the great advantage of a political environment that's very different from that of Agenda's last years, and even more so from that of the time when Agenda was founded. Participatory democracy, non-hierarchical organizing models, and other aspects of *how* we do our work are now widely understood as crucially interwoven with the politics of the work we do. Agenda's members are among those who have made that so, along with participants in groups like Movement for a New Society, ACT UP, the Direct Action Network, and the many projects inspired by the 1995 Zapatista uprising. The politics of Palestine and Zionism have shifted, as well, with the increasing polarization of U.S. Jewish communities between an unabashedly racist right and a rapidly growing non- and anti-Zionist left.[19] Agenda deserves a share of the credit for the early part of the leftward shift, along with the Jewish Women's Committee to End the Occupation and others.

The question we face now is which part of Agenda's legacy we want to bring with us as we move ahead: the one that urges us to see these two opportunities as integrally linked by a consistent focus on justice, or the one that urges us to deny those connections. Listening to Agenda's ghost can do more than help us understand why (and how and when) specifically Jewish radical organizing makes sense. It can also help us understand what genuinely radical political work can be.

---

19   For an overview and analysis, see for instance Daniel Lang/Levitsky, "Jews Confront Zionism" (available at http://monthlyreview.org/2009/06/01/jews-confront-zionism), and the sources cited within that article. Since that piece was written, U.S. Zionist 'peace'-oriented groups like Brit Tzedek v'Shalom, J Street, and the Tikkun Community have continued to decline in influence, visibility, and effectiveness, while non- and anti-Zionist projects from Jewish Voice for Peace to Jews Say No to the International Jewish Anti-Zionist Network have steadily grown in both size and strength.

Daniel Rosza Lang/Levitsky is a cultural worker, agitator, and archive excavator based in Crown Heights, Brooklyn. Just another enthusiastically secular, predictably bookish, 3rd-generation radical, 2nd-generation queer, presently somewhat-able-bodied, light-skinned ashkenazi, oysterlisher gendertreyf apikoyrus mischling fem with a love/hate relationship to identity terms. Jewishly: active in Jews For Racial & Economic Justice since 1999; co-founder of Jews Against the Occupation/ NYC; devoted militant of the Aftselokhes Ladies Auxiliary Spectacle Committee; admiring student of Adrienne Cooper zts"l and Jenny Romaine. Otherwise: core member of the NYC Direct Action Network and several of its descendent projects; dancer with the Rude Mechanical Orchestra; proud resident of Glitter House. Dos gezunt iz in dir / la salute é in voi.

APPENDICES

I. CALL FOR A 1980 CONGRESS OF PROGRESSIVE JEWS

Dear Friends,

An obvious vacuum exists today in the Jewish community. Despite the fact that American Jewry is highly organized, there is no forum in which the range of viewpoints characteristic of progressive Jews can be comfortably aired. While dissatisfied with the views of many Jewish spokespeople who claim to speak in our name, we have not found adequate alternatives.

Over a period of years some of us have thought, studied, and acted together, in a variety of contexts and organizations. We have grappled with issues and questions such as the following: How can we democratize the American Jewish community? How can we create a Jewish culture relevant to our own needs and time? How can support the legitimate needs of the Jewish communities abroad without subordinating or simplifying our own needs? How can we convince American Jewry that its long term survival may well be linked to support of progressive causes outside of the Jewish community? How can we convince non-Jewish progressives that the national liberation concerns of the Jewish People, in Israel and the Diaspora, must be part of the progressive agenda; that all too often in the recent past, progressives have not been sensitive to the unconscious anti-Semitism in some of their criticism of Jewish positions?

We are concerned about recent trends in the Jewish community to turn away from the struggle against injustice; to turn our energies into narrower channels. Too frequently the Jewish sage Hillel has been quoted: "If I am not for myself, then who will be for me?" without completing his teaching, "If I am only for myself, than what (value) and I?"

We therefore believe that the time is now (if not now, when?) to declare our criticism of the false dichotomy between "Jewish" issues and other concerns, between particularism and universalism. As Jews who believe strongly that authentic Jewishness can only be complete with serious and consistent attention to Tikun Olam (the just ordering of the physical world and human relationships), we believe it is time to join together in our commitment to work towards goals in the following areas:

I.   The American Jewish Community

Working toward democratizing American Jewish life and institutions. Building a healthy and viable culture drawn from the best of our religious traditions as well as rooted in the humanistic credo of the American Revolution. Strengthening Jewish family life through shared responsibility by men and women, shared power, extended communities, and especially quality Jewish education.

II.   Israel-Diaspora Relations and the Middle East

Supporting policies, as Jews and Americans, leading to lasting peace and true security for the State of Israel which we believe can only come about by finding a just solution for the Palestinian people. Working for a healthy Israel-Diaspora relationship that recognizes the integrity and interest of each, and supporting those forces within Israel working for an ethical, progressive nation, in the prophetic tradition.

III.   The World Community

Working toward a sane nuclear policy and the eradication of poverty in the developed and undeveloped world; elimination of socio-economic inequalities through affirmative action and other compensatory programs; elimination of discrimination against women through support of ERA; concern with the problems of the elderly in a culture which lacks respect for their position.

We do not yet have a collective response to these issues. We do, however, share a collective concern with them. If you share our concern, we hope you will join us in helping fill the vacuum in American Jewish life by working with us to create a progressive Jewish agenda for the 1980's. We are planning a Congress of Progressive Jews for next year, most likely in the fall; if interested, please fill out the form on the opposite side.

II: Dec 1980 Founding Conference
Unity Statement

New Jewish Agenda Chapter Handbook. 1981 (28)

We are Jews from a variety of backgrounds, affiliations, and personal outlooks who share a vision of the meaning and purpose of Jewish life. We have come together to explore and articulate that vision, to learn from one another, and to begin to translate our commitment into action. We believe that Jewish experience and teachings can address the social, economic, political issues of our time. Our Jewish conviction requires that we give serious and consistent attention to the Jewish mandate of *tikun olam*, the repair and moral improvement of our world.

It is not an easy time. American Jewry is fragmented, lacking leadership and eroded by assimilation. Israel is besieged, its economy collapsing, its hopes for peace fading. Anti-Semitism is everywhere on the rise, America remains a deeply troubled nation, unequal and confused, its new administration seemingly preparing for another era of repression, unlimited arms race, and destruction of the environment.

It is time for a New Jewish Agenda, a new understanding of Jewish responsibilities and possibilities for the 1980's, a new effort to apply Jewish values, traditions, and insights to our problems and needs.

We are committed to Jewish survival. Jews must have the rights to which every people are entitled: political independence and self-determination in Israel and full civil rights and cultural autonomy everywhere that Jews live. Survival, however, is only a precondition for Jewish life, not its purpose. Our agenda must be determined by our ethics, not our enemies.

We have come together to affirm the validity and vitality of progressive Jewish values at a time when many have lost faith that the goals of justice and peace are attainable. We believe that society can be improved and that human cooperation can be achieved. By working for social progress we not only reflect Jewish ideals, but ultimately enhance Jewish security as well.

We welcome to our cause any Jew who shares our visions, whether actively involved in the Jewish community or currently alienated from it. To those Jews whose goals differ from our own, we say: Let us join in dialogue. Let us achieve an authentic Jewish unity, one that grows not from forced unanimity, intolerance or the stifling of dissent, but from honest understanding and respect for diversity.

III. New Jewish Agenda National Platform

Adopted November 28, 1982

This platform was adopted at a Delegates Conference which took place in New York City and was attended by sixty-five elected representative of New Jewish Agenda chapters and at-large members from across the United States. The platform represents the climax of an extensive cooperative process that began at Agenda's Founding Conference in 1980. It represents our current political analysis with respect to the major issues of the day. We anticipate that it will be revised and amended as needed in the years to come.

Statement of Purpose

We are Jews from a variety of backgrounds and affiliations committed to progressive human values and the building of a shared vision of Jewish life.

Our history and tradition inspire us. Jewish experience and teachings can address the social, economic, and political issues of our time. Many of us find our inspiration in our people's historical resistance to oppression and from the Jewish presence at the forefront of movements for social change. Many of us base our convictions on the Jewish religious concept of *tikun olam* (the just ordering of human society and the world)1 and the prophetic traditions of social justice.

We are dedicated to insuring the survival and flourishing of the Jewish people. Jews must have the rights to which all people are entitled. But survival is only a precondition of Jewish life, not its purpose. Our agenda must be determined by our ethics, not our enemies. We need creative and vital Jewish institutions and practices that affirm the best of our traditions and involve members of our community who have historically been excluded.

We call on all Jews who share our vision to join us in working to achieve our goals in the Jewish and wider communities. To those whose visions differ from ours - let us discuss those differences. Authentic Jewish unity grows from respect for and understanding of diversity.

Society can be changed and human cooperation can be achieved. Working for social progress not only reflects Jewish ideals, but enhances Jewish security. New Jewish Agenda's national platform upholds progressive Jewish values and affirms that the goals of peace and justice are attainable.

Jewish Communal Life in the United States

New Jewish Agenda affirms the vitality and vast creative potential of Jewish life in the United States. We are proud of our historical tradition of providing for our educational, religious, social, cultural, and political news. However, the existing network of Jewish communal institutions has only partially succeeded in these tasks.

We call for the transformation of Jewish institutions and the creation of new ones to represent the whole spectrum of views of U.S. Jewry and meet our changing needs. Such democratic participatory structures will enhance the strength and depth of our communities.

1. We call for the full empowerment of all Jews. Our communal institutions must involve those whose needs have been consistently disregarded: our elders, Jews with disabilities, the poor, Lesbians and Gay Men. Jews not living in nuclear families, Jews of color, Jews by choice, those of mixed marriages, and recent immigrants.

2. All aspects of Jewish life, including leadership, must be shared equally by women and men.

3. Leadership should not be based on financial status. Such a practice is contrary to Jewish values and excludes creative individuals.

4. Affordable, quality Jewish education, encompassing religious and secular ideals, should be available for Jews of all ages. We support the development of non-sexist role models for our children.

5. Jewish institutions should be among those that are models of fair labor practices for both paid and unpaid work. Our community must recognize the value of volunteer work, especially that of women.

6. Open discussion of a broad range of views must be encouraged, not squelched. The Jewish press must fulfill its responsibility to report the full spectrum of facts and opinion, and to encourage debate.

7. We call for the reassertion of spirituality as the central component of our community's religious life, rather than the sterile institutionality that often predominates.

8. The *mitzvah* of *tzedakah* should no longer only refer to passive participation in a corporate fundraising enterprise, but must include meaningful activity towards providing for real needs and advancing social justice. Resources ought to be allocated democratically in our communities.

New Jewish Agenda's Feminist Commitment

New Jewish Agenda (NJA) supports the complete equality of women and men. Our policies are shaped by our commitment to feminism – an egalitarian system of thought and action. Human needs, interpersonal dynamics, and quality of life are political issues. In order to build NJA as a feminist organization, we emphasize cooperation, inclusive language, and the conscious affirmation of an egalitarian ethos.

Women's exclusion from power in society has resulted in pervasive economic social inequalities. This interferes with women's ability to reach economic stability, and frustrates all people's emotional fulfillment and creativity. Both men and women have suffered due to narrow concepts of masculinity and femininity, limiting our ability to be fully human. Our ways of relating to each other are constrained by these concepts, leading to a distortion of relationships between men and women and an irrational fear of same-sex relationships. The glorification of so-called "masculine" virtues of competition and aggression has contributed to the militarism which has brought the human race to the brink of self-destruction.

As feminists working in the Jewish community, we will work to bring women into positions of leadership, to reclaim women's true role in Jewish history, and to support the process of transforming our religious language and symbolism. As Jews working in the feminist community, we are dedicated to winning its active commitment to the unique struggle of Jewish women and to the struggle against anti-Semitism.

Women in the Work Force, Family, and Reproductive Rights

Women in the work force have historically faced poor conditions and inequitable compensation. We continue the struggle of our grand-mothers as we fight on the issue of our day.

We support equal pay for comparable worth. We oppose discrimina-tion in hiring and promotion against women, Lesbians and Gay Men. It is the employer's responsibility to provide child care, maternity and paternity leave and job sharing. These benefits are crucial to the redefinition of sex roles.

The workplace must be free from all health hazard, including those that affect the reproductive system. Women must be protected from sexual harassment. We support increasing unionization of clerical, childcare, and household workers and other predominantly female occupations.

We support programs which foster the autonomy of women and provide the economic and social grounding necessary for relationships of love and intimacy to grow. Families have been central to the con-tinued existence of the Jewish community. Today, political, economic and demographic changes demand that the concept of the family be expanded.

Any program which will strengthen the Jewish community must ac-knowledge the diversity of persons and household types that now ex-ist. This means abandoning the assumption that all Jews do, or ought, to live in nuclear or heterosexual families.

In light of this, New Jewish Agenda (NJA) opposes the "Family Pro-tection Act" and other legislation which attempt to recreate by force a "traditional" family form.
We affirm the value of life and the right of all children to be born into a loving and caring environment. Women should be free to choose when and under what conditions they bring life into the world. The question of a woman's right to have an abortion involves complex moral and religious issues. In the case of Jewish law, abortion is not only permitted but mandated in certain circumstances.2 NJA will fight

to retain safe, legal abortions and oppose depriving poor people of choices available to others.

We oppose all government policies limiting reproductive freedoms and affirm the right of children to be adequately cared for by society and by their parents. In order for prospective parents to be truly free in their choice, society must provide adequate child care, adequate incomes and housing. Full reproductive freedom also includes the access of individuals to safe and effective birth control, quality health education and medical services, the end to sterilization abuse and unnecessary reproductive surgery, and the rights of Lesbians, Gay Men, and single people to choose whether or not to parent, adopt, or retain custody.

Lesbians and Gay Jews

New Jewish Agenda supports the struggle of Lesbians and Gay Men to lead lives of freedom and dignity. We affirm this at a time when the Right is on the rise and when anti-Gay attacks are increasing. The scapegoating of Lesbians and Gay Men opens the way for the oppression of all minority groups, including Jews. Witness the fact that Lesbians and Gay Men were among the first and most brutally treated victims of the Holocaust.

Truly achieving Lesbian and Gay liberation necessitates freeing women and men from rigid sex role constraints, limitations on same-sex closeness, and narrowly defined family structures. We are committed to building an organization whose members are challenged in these areas and where Lesbians and Gay Men feel genuinely welcomed.

Lesbians and Gay Men are excluded from the dominant heterosexual culture. They suffer severe oppression, including physical assaults and denial of basic civil rights such as child custody. Homophobia (the irrational fear of Gay people, homosexuality, and same-sex closeness) permeates everyone's life.

The multiple oppression of being both Gay and Jewish makes the lives of Lesbian and Gay Jews more difficult. For example, preconceived images of the Jewish family put pressure on those who might not choose to marry. Anti-Semitic stereotypes of weak Jewish men and domineering Jewish women intersect with homophobic stereotypes of Gay Men as "weak and unmanly" and Lesbians as "masculine and anti-male." however, the ability of Lesbian and Gay Jews to draw from the richness and specialness of both their histories and cultures gives them unique perspective and creativity.

Jewish religious tradition has neither condoned homosexuality nor accepted Lesbians and Gay Men as equal participants in Jewish communal life. However, Judaism is evolving, as evidenced by changes in women's roles. We reject the anti-Gay rights position of some Jews and Jewish organizations as antithetical to our Jewish heritage of respect for human rights. We urge the involvement of all Jews in the struggle for full civil rights for Lesbians and Gay Men, and welcome ongoing dialogue within the Jewish community about the relationship between traditions Jewish beliefs and the goals of Lesbian and Gay liberation.

Jews with Disabilities

As part of our commitment to include all Jews in the life of our community, we in New Jewish Agenda call attention to concerns of those in our midst who have physical, mental, emotional, or learning disabilities. We draw from that part of our tradition that affirms the unique worth of all individuals, and reject traditional attitudes of exclusion or ambivalence toward people with disabilities. We recognize the importance of overcoming stigmas about disabilities.

All Jewish organizations ought to be fully accessible in architecture, communication and attitudes. The lack of visibility and involvement of Jews with disabilities deprives our community of valuable participants.

We in New Jewish Agenda support the civil and economic rights of all people with disabilities. We will work towards making our own organizational events fully accessible.

Anti-Semitism

Anti-Semitism is prejudice against or persecution of Jews as a people. It can take the form of religious and cultural suppression, economic and educational discrimination, denial of political rights, expulsion, and even genocide. Although we have survived for thousands of years, we are still not free from oppression. A central goal of New Jewish Agenda is to end anti-Semitism.

Economic, political, and social restrictions have historically isolated Jews, often placing us in a buffer role, as "middle-men" between the more powerful social classes and the oppressed (for example, tax-collectors in medieval Poland). This role has often been a pretext for anti-Semitism. Thus an entire people has been scapegoated for the faults of an oppressive social system.

Social and economic justice is necessary but not sufficient for the eradication of anti-Semitism. Anti-Semitism has a life of its own and must be confronted directly.

Racial hatred against Jews fueled the Nazi rise to power, culminating in the Holocaust. We mourn our dead and the psychic scarring of our people. Understanding the causes and lesson of this ultimate act of anti-Semitism involves educating ourselves and others – without sensationalizing, trivializing, or focusing on it as the only significant event in Jewish history, or as the basis of our Jewishness. We are proud that our people survived, and celebrate Jewish heroism and resistance.

The legacy of persecution has left Jews with deep anxiety about survival. Jews have been forced to either assimilate into the dominant culture, or to isolate themselves in fear and suspicion of non-Jews. Many have sought individual economic security as a solution. These responses have been ineffective in ending anti-Semitism.

As the world economic crisis deepens, we are confronted with a rise of overt anti-Semitic incidents. Bombings have occurred in Paris and Rome. Swastikas have appeared on college campuses, synagogues, and Jewish-owned property in the U.S. Anti-Semitism is also evident when Israel is judged by standards different than those used for other countries, or when all Jews are held responsible for Israeli government actions.

As a key to ending Jewish oppression, we in NJA will make alliances with other oppressed groups on the basis of mutual respect and struggle. We are devoted to building a strong, proud Jewish identity.

Racism

New Jewish Agenda strongly opposes institutional and individual racism. Our ongoing struggle against racism, both within and outside the Jewish community, stems from our own experience of racial bigotry, our traditional commitment to social justice, and our awareness that any division of peoples is harmful to all.

Racism has been used by those in power to maintain their own economic and political positions, and to divide their opposition. It is an integral part of the functions of our economic system. For example, people of color have provided a cheap and exploitable work force, drawn from a pool of underemployed and unemployed labor.

In the 1980's, as the U.S. faces continuing economic deterioration, people of color are among those hardest hit by rising unemployment and cutbacks in social services. At the same time, there has been a dangerous resurgence of Klan and Nazi violence, and other forms of racism such as police brutality, harassment of undocumented workers, violation of Native American rights, and opposition to school integration.

We are also concerned about the stereotyping and discrimination against Arabs and Arab-Americans that is widespread through the United States. The Arab-Israeli conflict does not oblige Jews to accept this negative view of Arabs and Islam.

The growing rift between Jews and Blacks is both painful and important to confront. Short-range economic and social conflicts of interest have opened the door to all forms of bigotry. Both Jews and Blacks are hurt by this rift which weakens the fights against anti-Semitism and racism.

We resolve to help build broad-based coalitions in which Blacks, Hispanics, Asians, Native Americans, other ethnic minorities, labor groups, and progressive political organizations will work together to fight racism. In building these alliances, we will seek to end Jewish isolation and foster mutual respect for the goals of all people.

Affirmative Action

We support affirmative action as one method of redressing discrimination against women, people of color, economically disadvantaged and disabled people.

We support the use of minimum quotas to achieve equality in certain circumstances. The system of minimum quotas is fundamentally different from the system of maximum quotas that has been used against Jews. Maximum quotas establish a ceiling on the participation of Jews and others in social and economic life. They are a barrier to social equality. We would oppose any mistaken interpretation of minimum affirmative action quotas as maximum hiring quotas.

Affirmative action is of direct assistance to more than 50% of the Jewish community: women, Jews of color, economically disadvantaged and disabled Jews.

While we support affirmative action programs, we also acknowledge their limitations, as they do not focus on the right of every individual to a job, to full access to educational institutions, and to better living conditions. Affirmative actions is only one aspect of the broader movement for social and economic equality.

Civil Liberties

Having suffered the devastating effects of persecution and prejudice, Jews can play a special role in defense of freedom and democratic rights. The U.S. Constitution pledges that all people are equal and assures due process, freedom of speech, and the free exercise of religion. These liberties now face ever-growing challenges.

1. New Jewish Agenda opposes efforts to increase government secrecy, reinstitute Congressional inquisitorial activities, limit personal privacy or sanction political spying by intelligence-gathering agencies. We challenge the view that "national security" is more important than the Bill of Rights.

2. NJA decries attempts to control crime and violence by such means as limits of due process, preventive detention, and capital punishment. Justice and compassion, basic to our tradition, should be the foundation of efforts to restore "law and order."

3. The "Moral Majority" threatens constitutional freedom and the separation of church and state. Their attempts to put prayer back in the schools and to teach so-called "Christian morality" are an attack on basic religious liberties for all minorities including Jews. These groups threaten the rights of women, Lesbians, Gay Men, and work against Jewish interests. We oppose coalitions with such groups based solely on their support for Israel.

4. Undocumented works in the U.S. continually face denial of basic civil liberties. As Jews, with a recent immigrant experience and a concern for the stranger dating back to Biblical times, we strongly oppose such policies. Immigrants should not be scapegoats for economic injustice. During the Holocaust thousands of Jews were denied refuge from Nazism. Political refugees, whose lives are often in danger in their homelands, should be able to enter and remain in this country.

NJA opposed the misuse of legitimate issues like national security, law and order, and morality, to institutionalize conservative social and economic policies. In this time of economic crisis, the Right's attack on civil liberties deflects attention from the fundamental need to reorder society.

Energy and Environment

U.S. energy and environmental policy should promote full employment, affordability, protection of the environment, conservation of natural resources, health and safety, and democracy. These principles are in full accord with traditional Jewish values, which recognize that the responsible use of the earth and its resources is essential to the quality of human life.

We advocate a transition to a publicly owned, community-based, energy system relying on renewable energy sources, conservation and recycling. Such a system can provide employment and local control, and be a powerful tool for economic development. In the meantime we must rely on energy efficient, small-scale power generation, and methods of using fossil fuels which minimize their environmental impact.

Because of its unique dangers, high economic costs, centralized control, and role in facilitating nuclear proliferation, we oppose the use of nuclear energy. The independence and accountability of public regulatory agencies and commissions must be ensured. Proper enforcement of public safety standards and establishment of equitable utility rates and rate structures can only be guaranteed by dissolving the "revolving door" relationship that often exists among public officials and energy companies.

Public policy must also provide for the right of all people to necessary heating and cooling through adequate fuel assistance programs. Private enterprise, guided solely by profits, leaves it to the public to bear the true costs of pollution. The Federal government must therefore maintain its responsibility to regulate air and water quality and the disposal of toxic wastes. Nevertheless, local governments should have the right to enact stricter regulations.

The U.S. Government also must work with other nations to ensure the proper protection of the international environment. Workers suffer the highest exposure to toxic substances. They and their representative unions have the right to knowledge of and protection from these dangers. Communities surrounding potential sources of toxic pollution are entitled to know what substances are produced, stored or handled there. Both workers and communities harmed by exposure to toxic substances are entitled to full restitution for any physical harm or property damage.

Economic Justice

Jewish tradition holds human welfare in high esteem. Property rights never take precedence over human rights. Care for those who cannot care for themselves is an act of justice to which the recipient is entitled by virtue of being human. The United States economy is not providing for human needs.

In the U.S. today the economic system is facing a crisis similar in scope to that of the 1930's. The results of the economic crisis are declines in profit rates, stagnation or decline in most people's spending power, and most importantly, a sharp rise in the unemployment rate. Current economic policy seeks to restore corporate profit rates by redistributing income from working people and the poor to the rich. Our beliefs are exactly opposed to the Reagan program of tax benefits for business and the wealthy.

New Jewish Agenda calls for a program of economic democracy to benefit the majority, not just the wealthy minority. We support full, fair, and safe employment and provision for the needs of the elderly, people with disabilities, and all those unable to work. This can only be accomplished through a system of democratic planning. Under today's conditions we support thorough reform of the tax system to eliminate loopholes and subsidies for the rich and a massive transfer of resources from military to civilian needs. Public programs should support urban reconstruction, public transportation, education, health, child care and the arts.

The Labor Movement

The New Jewish Agenda includes among its constituency many Jews for whom the American labor movement is of primary political and economic importance. Today, Jews, along with other minorities, are in the forefront of one of the most important segments of the trade union movement: public sector and human services.

Labor is in retreat in both the economic and political arenas. Capital flight has eroded labor's traditional industrial base. This threat serves as a hindrance to organizing due to a real fear of job loss. The lack of labor law reform and the present restrictive labor legislation not only impedes organizing, but also restricts the power of unions to engage in meaningful collective bargaining. The current economic crisis exacerbates this situation. The narrow focus on pecuniary benefits further impedes labor's growth. In order to grow, labor needs to reassert itself as a democratically led social movement. Women and minority workers represent the largest source of potential union members. To attract these workers, unions must meet their specific needs.

The quality of our lives is closely tied to the success of the labor movement. Social programs such as public education, social security, and subsidized housing owe their existence to the efforts of organized labor. At the workplace, the collective bargaining agreement remains the only real protection workers have. We look to organized labor as a vehicle of potential power initiating and implementing broad social and economic change.

Relations Between Israel and North American Jewry

New Jewish Agenda upholds the traditions that *kol yisrael areivim zeh b'zeh*, all Jews are responsible one for another. Our histories, traditions, values, and sentiments have created a connection between us and the Jewish State of Israel. We believe that the fate of the Jewish people in one part of the world is linked to the fate of the Jewish people in other parts of the world.

Israeli and North American Jews share a concern for each other's secure future and ethical character. Decisions about Israel's life and policy must be made by the Israelis, just as we must make decision affecting North American Jewish life. Nonetheless, we recognize our relations as one of mutual responsibility, including the obligation to address each other's weaknesses as well as strengths. To fail to speak in candor is to decline this responsibility and to imply that we do not care.

We affirm the right and necessity of Jews everywhere to engage in democratic debate and open discussion regarding Israeli policies. As progressive Jews, we in New Jewish Agenda identify with the Jewish historical emphasis on peace and social justice and support those in Israel who are working toward these goals.

Internal Social Life in Israel

We want to work towards an Israel based on the best of Jewish tradition and ideals of social justice. We celebrate many of Israel's accomplishments – in democratic processes, nation-building, and social and economic development. We are committed to Israel as a society in which Arabs and Jews, Sephardim, Edot HaMizrach and Ashkenazim, women and men, and secular and religious people of all persuasions can cooperate and contribute fully and equally.

We support the principles of the Declaration of Independence of the State of Israel, which vows "to uphold the full social and political equality of all its citizens, without distinction of religion, race, or sex," and "to guarantee freedom of religion, conscience, education, and culture."

We support progressive forces in Israel who, in this spirit, are working to achieve the following goals:

1. Elimination of social and economic discrimination against the Sephardic-Mizrachi majority and Arab, Druze, and other minority groups;

2. Equal educational opportunities regardless of cultural, religious, and ethnic backgrounds;

3. Equal rights for women, including equal pay for comparable work and full reproductive rights;

4. An end to the Orthodox monopoly on religious organization and to religious control in civic affairs;

5. An end to discrimination against Lesbians and Gay Men, including removal of the restrictions in the Israel Law of Return regarding sexual preference;

6. Insuring freedom of the press and expression and easing of military censorship laws;

7. The adoption of a Constitution, incorporating a Bill of Rights, which would take precedence over religious and military law and extend to all individuals living under Israeli law the basic rights delineated in the Universal Declaration of Human Rights;

8. The development of a dialogue between Arabs and Jews as a prelude to reconciliation of the two communities; and

9. An end to the continued occupation and drive to annex the territories. The occupation is polarizing and corrupting Israeli society, undermining its democracy, and has led to repression and an increasing infringement of basic rights of those living in the territories.

Israel, The Palestinians and Arab Neighbors

After decades of hatred and bloodshed, it is clear that there can be no peace in the Middle East without a political resolution of the conflict among Israelis, Palestinians, and the Arab states. For many Jews, Israel represents the fulfillment of a dream of an independent homeland, and a refuge from centuries of persecution in many lands. The Palestinians have also been exiled, dispersed, denied their rights, and have been kept from establishing political sovereignty in a land of their own. Regardless of how either side views the "historical legitimacy" of the other, both Israeli Jews and Palestinian Arabs are in the Middle East to stay.

Our Concern as Jews

As Jews committed to the existence of Israel, we recognize that peace between Israel and its Arab neighbors is essential to Israel's survival. The continuing state of war and military rule over another people diminishes the prospects for Israel's long-term viability. We believe that Israel cannot rule over the Palestinians as an occupying force without degrading the Jewish and human ideals which served as a basis for Israel's creation. A key to the solution of the Arab-Israeli conflict is compromise between Israeli and Palestinian nationalisms. It is not possible to solve this conflict through military means.

Principles of Peace

We believe that to be successful and lasting, a comprehensive settlement must embody the following principles:

1. The Jewish people's right to national self-determination in the State of Israel.
2. National self-determination for the Palestinian people.
3. Mutual recognition and peaceful relations among Israel, the Arab states, and the Palestinians.
4. Withdrawal by Israel from territories occupied since June 5, 1967.
5. Guarantees for Israeli security with recognized borders and mutually agreed-upon provisions responding to the fears and real security needs of all concerned parties.

Toward These End, We Join With Israelis and Other in Calling For:

1. Renunciation by all parties of all violence, including terrorism, as means to achieve their aims.

2. Recognition by the Arab states and the Palestine Liberation Organization (P.L.O.) of the right of the State of Israel to exist within secure and recognized borders.

3. Recognition by the State of Israel of the right of Palestinians to national self-determination, including the right to the establishment, if they so choose, of an independent and viable Palestinian state in the West Bank and Gaza, and an end to the repression of the Palestinians.

4. Direct negotiations between Israel and legitimate representatives of the Palestinian people, including the P.L.O., on the basis of mutual recognition and a commitment to peaceful co-existence.

Israel and the International Community

The continued hostilities among Israel, the Arab countries and the Palestinians are fueled by the rivalry between the United States and the Soviet Union. This rivalry has given rise to a spiraling arms race by the superpowers in the area and continuing direct and indirect intervention into the internal affairs of all states in the Middle East. It has encouraged the channeling of vital human and economic resources into a quest for military supremacy, and has led to repeated military conflicts which could easily result in nuclear war.

While an adequate defense force is necessary for Israel's security, we are alarmed at the increasing militarization of Israeli society, the use of U.S.-supplied arms for territorial expansion, and the interference in the internal life of neighboring countries.

Israel also violates our sense of Jewish ethics when it sells arms to repressive dictatorships in Latin America, South Africa, and elsewhere. Such policies increase Israel's isolation. We urge Israel to stop all such arms sales.

U.S., Soviet, and other arms exports to Arab countries buttress repressive, undemocratic regimes and thus continue to threaten Israel's survival.

We believe that a lasting peace in the Middle East can only be achieved through mutually satisfactory agreements among all parties directly involved in the conflict. We call upon the United States to take the initiative with the Soviet Union in working toward an international agreement to arms reduction in the region.

Policies which strive to base Israel's security solely on a strategic alliance with the United States increase Israel's isolation, threaten detente, and are therefore not in Israel's long-term interest. A comprehensive peace settlement is a necessary first step to returning Israel to a position of non-alignment in the superpower conflict.

World Jewry and Threatened Jewish Communities

United by history, language, and cultures which transcend political boundaries, the Jewish people is composed of many communities dispersed over the world. New Jewish Agenda believes that the continued existence of diverse Jewish communities is essential to a flourishing Jewish life. Our common bond demands our moral, economic, and organizational commitment to the welfare of all Jewish communities. Many of these communities face a variety of threats. Among those most seriously threatened are the Jewish communities of: the Soviet Union, Syria, Iran, Ethiopia and Argentina. NJA is now focusing on three areas of grave concern.

Soviet Jews

NJA firmly supports the struggle of Soviet Jews to achieve basic cultural, religious, and human rights as Jews. We support all attempts to allow Jews who choose to emigrate to other countries to do so freely without undue hardship. The Soviet government must honor the international right to freedom of movement and must implement its stated guarantees of cultural and civil right to Jews, other minority peoples, and all its citizens.

Ethiopian Jews

The Beta Yisroel, the Jews of Ethiopia, face a threat to their existence due to war, famine, and persecution. Those Jews who desire to leave should be allowed to do so and should receive whatever assistance is necessary from World Jewry. To those who wish to remain, the Ethiopian government must guarantee freedom from religious oppression.

Past rescue efforts of this Black Jewish community by the Israeli government and the Jewish Agency have been clearly insufficient and do not reflect a sense of urgency. The failure to save those who are suffering and dying in refugee camps scattered throughout the Horn of Africa, and more accessible to rescue efforts, is particularly egregious.

Official rescue efforts have only occurred in response to pressure from segments of World Jewry and the Ethiopian Jewish community in Israel. This pressure has to be continued and expanded.

Argentine Jews

Argentine Jewry, the largest Jewish community in Latin America, is in danger. The bombing of Jewish communal institutions, the wide dissemination of Nazi literature, and the use of Nazi symbols by prison officials are manifestations of the growth of open anti-Semitism. Jewish political prisoners often are singled out for especially harsh forms of torture.

We oppose the massive violations of human rights of Argentine citizens, Jewish and non-Jewish. We support human rights activists in Argentina who call for the "re-appearance with life" of the 30,000 "desaparecidos" or disappeared people. The Argentine government must release its political prisoners. To that end, American Jewry must bring pressure upon American and Argentine officials.

Militarism and the Nuclear Arms Race

The injunctions "Choose life" and "Seek peace" have long been central doctrines of Jewish ethics.3 Their fulfillment is threatened by the escalation of militarism throughout the world.

The United States and the Soviet Union have initiated and shaped current global military policy, causing diversion of human and material resources from socially constructive purposes to the development and acquisition of weapons. In the effort to maximize profits, the U.S. weapons industry has been a powerful force in shaping a foreign policy that supports political repression in the Third World, promotes belligerency between neighbors, and causes economic deprivations in the United States and abroad. These burdens fall most heavily on Third World countries where over-expenditures on weapons leave people facing greater illiteracy, malnutrition, and disease. Furthermore, militarizing of the world economy has been a fundamental cause of worldwide inflation.

We urge that funds presently used for military expenditures be redirected to meet human needs and we support the economic conversion of military production to labor-intensive industries for peaceful purposes.

Draft registration and induction serve as preparations for war and should be opposed. We support all those who refuse involvement in actions which further military activities. We advocate a legal form of military tax redirection for those conscientious objectors who must presently engage in illegal war-tax resistance. People who have "selective objection" to certain wars should be granted C.O. [Conscientious Objector] status. In light of the support for conscientious objection within Jewish tradition, we specifically urge Israel to recognize the rights of C.O.'s.

The existence of chemical and biological weapons threaten human lives and the environment by completely altering entire ecosystems. We call for the cessation of further research, development and use of these weapons.

We call for a halt to the export of nuclear power technology by the U.S. and other western nations in order to stem the proliferation of nuclear weapons, we further oppose the development of nuclear breeder technology which would represent a commitment to a plutonium-based U.S. economy.

The unrelenting emphasis on military supremacy now threatens us with the horror of nuclear conflagration. Jews have experienced one holocaust in this century; we cannot sit idly by while preparations are being made for the ultimate holocaust.

We call for universal nuclear disarmament as a step towards establishing world peace.

We call on all nations to renounce the concept of a limited nuclear war which serves to justify the development of first-strike weapons. We support proposals to create nuclear weapons-free zones, particularly in the Middle East.

The two superpowers have consistently undermined arms control efforts; both parties must immediately enter serious negotiations. To begin this process, we support a bilateral freeze agreement between the U.S. and the U.S.S.R. to halt the development, production, testing, and deployment of all nuclear weapons systems. We strongly support the efforts of those working for nuclear disarmament in the U.S. and the U.S.S.R., and throughout the world.

As Jews, we honor the obligation to cherish the earth and care for its people. We call on the entire Jewish community to join us in the campaign to reverse the arms race so that human needs will be met.

IV. A SECTION FROM "LESSONS LEARNED IN ORGANIZING AMERICAN JEWS" BY CHERIE BROWN.

Tikkun 16:4. July/August 2001

Overcoming Isolation to Become Effective

1981. The New Jewish Agenda, founded in this year, was one of the best progressive Jewish organizations that we ever launched. The goal of New Jewish Agenda was to be a "progressive voice in the Jewish community and a Jewish voice in the progressive community." After all the brutal attacks on the leadership of Breira, New Jewish Agenda decided that the policies of the Israeli government would never be challenged successfully without a multi-issue Jewish organization in the United States that could help American Jews break through their Israel-only politics.

However, two weeks before the founding convention of New Jewish Agenda, I started getting urgent phone calls every day from Jewish activists all over the United States. The founding conference had not even taken place yet, but many had already decided that the meeting could not possibly come up with left-enough politics, so they were organizing to set up another fringe caucus! Instead of joining forces and building a unified coalition, these Jewish activists were recreating the all too familiar feeling of isolation by attacking the conference agenda, deciding it would not be left enough, Jewish enough, etc.

New Jewish Agenda was a response, in part, to the attacks from mainstream Jewry on Breira. But what ultimately killed NJA, in my opinion, were not the attacks from the outside, but the attacks on leadership from within the organization. The staff was never completely trusted. Weakened by ongoing bickering and attacks from within, Agenda finally folded.

What did I learn from New Jewish Agenda? That progressive Jews who have functioned in isolation for so long, when given an opportunity to form a national coalition with other like-minded Jews, will find any excuse to recreate the same isolation. For many, it is just too unbearable to imagine that there is an alternative to functioning on the fringes of the Jewish community. However, we cannot build an effective campaign to end the occupation without a strong commitment to support the leadership of that campaign. The leadership must know that they have a mandate to lead – and not be afraid to be creative, to take risks when needed, and to apply the organization's principles in circumstances where there has not yet been time to talk everything out.

In short, ultra-democracy can paralyze effective organizing. Needing a decision from every member before any action can be taken hamstrings the leadership, slows action to a standstill, and ends up watering down the activism to the lowest common denominator. The reality is that many people participating in such an "ultra democracy" process end up feeling *more alienated* and less inclined to stay part of the movement.

V. Why NJA Disbanded: Letters

Tikkun.16:5 (Sept/Oct 2001)

To the Editor:

At a time when we're seeing a resurgence of progressive Jewish organizing, it's helpful to understand why previous efforts waned. The ones with which we're most familiar took place in the 1980s within the context of New Jewish Agenda (NJA). While Cherie Brown identifies in-fighting and lack of support for leadership as the causes of NJA's demise ("Lessons Learned in Organizing American Jews," Tikkun July/August 2001), as former national cochair and executive director, we can attest that the reasons were far more complex.

First, it's important to recount NJA's successes. Begun in 1980 as a multi-issue progressive organization, NJA raised consciousness about nuclear disarmament, racism and anti-Semitism, lesbian and gay liberation, U.S. policy in Central America, and Israeli-Palestinian reconciliation. NJA introduced many American Jews to the Israeli peace movement and to Palestinians for the first time. It educated local Jewish communities about a two-state solution and the need to negotiate with the PLO, during a time when uttering those words was considered heretical in some circles.

While no one has offered a definitive explanation as to why NJA closed its doors in 1992, one would have to include these factors:

1. Dual focus: NJA was created to be a Jewish voice among progressives and a progressive voice among Jews. This had strengths and weaknesses. At best, it led to strategies that were flexible and creative; at worst it led to chronic disagreements about who we intended to organize and how – perhaps the in-fighting to which Brown refers. Although some of these vigorous debates may have been unnecessary, others were about valid political differences that still exist among progressive Jews.

2. Organizational culture: While other national progressive organizations turned their attention away from the grassroots and toward

the Beltway, NJA remained committed to grassroots organizing and a vision of participatory democracy. Again, this had both strengths and weaknesses. It engaged many activists who had previously been excluded from Jewish communal politics, including women, lesbians and gay men, working class Jews, and others, giving us a Jewish and political home. At the same time, NJA's organizational culture demanded a lot of members, decision making was slow, and potential supporters were alienated. NJA's organizational culture resulted in chronic underfunding, and ultimately the organization exhausted its resources.

3. Sister organizations: NJA's existence supported the development of a number of single-issue progressive organizations during the 1980s. These included American Friends of Peace Now, New Israel Fund, Jewish Fund for Justice, The Shalom Center, The Shefa Fund, *Bridges* magazine, and others. NJA's radical edge paved the way for other groups to organize a more mainstream constituency. In addition, NJA served as an informal training ground for many who became staff and leaders of these organizations. There came a point in the late 1980s when it appeared that single-issue groups were gaining steam and NJA was not needed as much. If creating a sense of possibility and an infrastructure for progressive Jewish politics is any measure, NJA was surely a victim of its own success.

Would we want to build a new organization in the likeness of New Jewish Agenda? No way! We live in a new era, one in which the challenges and opportunities facing the Jewish community, the Left, and the world are vastly different than those of the 1980s. But understanding where NJA succeeded and where it failed will help put the next wave of organizing on more solid ground.

Christie Balka
Philadelphia, PA

Reena Bernards
Chevy Chase, MD

Bibliography

"10,000 Protesters Denounce Reagan" *New Amsterdam News: The New Black View* (New York, NY) March 27, 1982. http://newjewishagenda.wordpress.com/?attachment_id=136

"250-300 Jewish Protesters Relieve Christian Colleagues at Rally Against Apartheid in South Africa." *Jewish Telegraphic Agency*, Dec 27 1984.

"American Jewish Year Book Archive Volume 85 (1985)." American Jewish Committee. Accessed December 20, 2011. http://www.ajcarchives.org/AJC_DATA/Files/1985_4_USCivicPolitical.pdf.

"American Jewish Year Book Archive Volume 86 (1986)." American Jewish Committee. Accessed December 20, 2011. www.ajcarchives.org/AJC_DATA/Files/1986_13_DirectoriesLists.pdf.

Balka, Christie. Interview by author. Personal interview. Philadelphia, PA, August 23, 2004.

Balka, Christie and Reena Bernards. Letter. *Tikkun*.16:5 (Sept/Oct 2001): 4. Accessed October 12, 2011. http://www.tikkun.org/article.php?story=sep2001_tikkun2.

Beck, Evelyn Torton. *Nice Jewish Girls: A Lesbian Anthology*. Boston: Beacon Press, 1989.

Becker, Aliza. " To Israel and back again | The Christian Century." *The Christian Century*. Accessed October 12, 2011. http://www.christiancentury.org/article/2002-02/israel-and-back-again

Bernards, Reena. Interview by author. Personal interview. Silver Springs, MD, July 8, 2004.

"Bernards Reflects on Nairobi Women's Conference" *The American Israelite*. April 24, 1986.

Blankfort, Jeffrey. "Proposition W and The Pacification of the U.S. Middle East Movement." Palestine: Information with Provenance. Accessed October 12, 2011. http://student.cs.ucc.ie/cs1064/jabowen/IPSC/articles/article0018834.html

Bloch, Ethan D. "ONE VOICE LESS FOR THE JEWISH LEFT: NEW JEWISH AGENDA 1981 - 1993" Essay shared with author on May 9, 2008. http://newjewishagenda.files.wordpress.com/2012/01/ethan-bloch.pdf

Bresler, Joyce. "Toward a Progressive World View." NJA Newsletter #10, Summer 1982: 5.

Brettschneider, Marla. *Cornerstones of Peace: Jewish Identity Politics and Democratic Theory.* New Brunswick, NJ: Rutgers Univ Press, 1996.

Brodkin, Karen. *How Jews Became White Folks and What That Says About Race in America.* New Brunswick, NJ: Rutgers University Press, 1998.

Brown, Cherie R. "American Jewish Activism; Lessons Learned In Organizing American Jews For Peace In The Middle East," 2002, *Brit Tzedek v'Shalom*, Accessed October 12, 2011. http://btvshalom.org/conference/founding/brown.shtml

---."Lessons Learned in Organizing American Jews." *Tikkun* 16:4 (2001): 13. Accessed October 12, 2011. http://www.tikkun.org/article.php/jul2001_brown

Bulkin, Elly. *Enter Password: Recovery.* Albany, NY: Turtle Books, 1990.

Bulkin, Elly, Minnie Bruce Pratt, and Barbara Smith. *Yours in Struggle: Three Feminist Perspectives on Antisemitism and Racism.* Ithaca, NY: Firebrand Books, 1988.

Chazanov, Mathis. "Jewish Activists Urge Synagogues to Shelter Latin American Refugees." *Los Angeles Times.* Nov 22, 1984. http://newjewishagenda.wordpress.com/?attachment_id=131

Cohen, Debra Nussbaum. "Behind the Headlines; Candidate Fulani Represents a Party Criticized As Deceptive, Anti-semitic." *Jewish Telegraphic Agency.* Jan 7 1992.

Coyne, David. "Memorandum re: the New Alliance Party." Dec 18, 1987.

Dekro, Jeffrey. Interview by author. Phone interview. July 9, 2004.

Deverey, Michael. "Defeat of Racism Resolution Seen as 'Victory.'"

The Kansas City Jewish Chronicle. Nov 15, 1985.

Ehrlich, Deborah. "New Jewish Agenda Convention Urges Recognition of PLO." MERIP, Oct.-Dec. 1985. http://newjewishagenda. files.wordpress.com/2011/11/convention20urges20recogn-20plo. pdf

Elkin, Judith Laikin. *The Jews of Latin America.* New York: Holmes & Meier, 1998.

"Federation Accepts New Jewish Agenda." *Jewish Messenger.* July 6. 1984. http://newjewishagenda.wordpress.com/?attachment_ id=190

Fellman, Gordon. Interview by author. Phone interview. July 8, 2004.

Freeman, Kevin. "Reagan Denounces the 'obscenity of Anti-semitism and Racism' and Reaffirms U.S. Commitment to Israel." *Jewish Telegraphic Agency.* Mar 25, 1982.

Fischman, Dennis. "Let My People In! Jewish Activist Urges Support from Progressives." *Critical Times.* http://newjewishagenda.word-press.com/?attachment_id=182

Friedman, David. "At a Succah in Washington: Several Hundred People Rally to Protest Against the Funding, Development,." *Jewish Telegraphic Agency*, Oct 15 1984.

---."Sukkat Shalom: Jews Seek to End Nuclear Arms Race." *Jewish Exponent.* October 19, 1984. http://newjewishagenda.wordpress. com/?attachment_id=130

Gould, Deborah B. "Life during Wartime: Emotions and the Development of ACT UP," *Mobilization* 7: 2. 2002: 1 – 27.

Grann, David. "Newman and Fulani: The Infiltrators." Lyndon Larouche Watch - Lyndon Larouche - Lenora Fulani - Fred Newman Unmasked. Accessed October 12, 2011. http://lyndonlarouche-watch.org/infiltrators.htm.

Haddad, Carol. Letter of critique from Feminist Arab Network. July 1 1985. http://newjewishagenda.wordpress.com/?attachment_ id=174.

Hyer, Marjorie. "Jewish Group Finds No Anti-Semitism by Sandanista Regime" *The Washington Post.* Aug 25, 1984. http://newjewishagenda.wordpress.com/?attachment_id=128

Isaac, Rael Jean. *Breira: Counsel for Judaism.* New York: Americans for a Safe Israel, 1977.

---. New Jewish Agenda: Dissent or Disloyalty. New York: Americans for a Safe Israel, 1989.

---. The anti New Jewish Agenda. New York: Americans for a Safe Israel, 1987.

Joffe, Mark. "Jews Join Thousands in Rally for Peace." *Jewish Exponent.* June 18, 1982. http://newjewishagenda.wordpress.com/?attachment_id=119

Kaiser, Jo Ellen Green. "The Roundtable' Is Offered A Seat: Social Justice Groups To Have Strong Presence at G.A." *The Jewish Daily Forward.* August 13, 2010. http://www.forward.com/articles/129833/

Kaye/Kantrowitz, Melanie. *The Issue is Power: Essays on Women, Jewish, Violence and Resistance.* San Francisco: Aunt Lute Books, 1992.

Kaye/Kantrowitz, Melanie and Irena Klepfisz, eds. *The Tribe of Dina: A Jewish Women's Anthology.* Boston: Beacon Press, 1989.

Klepfisz, Irena. *Dreams of a Insomniac: Jewish Feminist Essays, Speeches, and Diatribes.* Portland, OR: Eighth Mountain Press, 1990.

Kinberg, Clare. Interview by author. Phone interview. July 9, 2004.

---."The Challenge of Difference at Bridges." *In The Narrow Bridge: Jewish Views on Multiculturalism,* edited by Marla Brettschneider. New Brunswick, NJ: Rutgers Univ Press, 1996. 27-41.

Kivel, Paul. "I'm Not White I'm Jewish: Standing as Jews in the Fight for Racial Justice." PaulKivel.com. Accessed Oct 12, 2011. www.paulkivel.com/resources/articles/item/74-im-not-white-im-jewish-standing-as-jews-in-the-fight-for-racial-justice.

Kramer, Larry. *Reports from the Holocaust: The Making of an AIDS activist.* New York: St. Martin's Press, 1989.

Lehrer, Chaia. "A Lesbian Looks at Outreach." *Gesher Newsletter* 1:3 (October 1986), 3.

Lehrer, Joanne. *Jews, Justice and Community: An Analysis of Radical Jewish-Identified Organizing in the United States. 1880-1995.* Division III Thesis. Hampshire College, 1995: 71.

Light, Nancy. "At the UN Women's Conference: Final Forward-Looking Document Adopted Without Any Explicit Reference to Zionism or Israel." *JTA Daily News Bulletin.* July 29, 1985.

"March Called a Success." Jewish Week of Maryland, Virginia and Washington DC. Sept 1-7, 1983. http://newjewishagenda.word-press.com/?attachment_id=179.

Mark, Jonathan. "Toward a New Jewish Agenda: The Left's Last Chance." *New Jewish Times.* Feb/March 1981: 23-26.

Milner, Jenney and Donna Spiegelman. "Carrying It On: a Report from the NJA Convergence on Organizing Against Racism and Anti-Semitism." *Bridges Journal* 3:1 (Spring/Summer 1992): 138-147.

Moroze, Lewis. "New Jewish Agenda: A Welcome Voice." Political Affairs 60, no. 4 (1981): 30-36. http://newjewishagenda.files.wordpress.com/2011/11/nja-a-welcome-voice.pdf

"New Jewish Agenda Folds its Tent." *Bridges Journal.* 4:1 (Winter/Spring 1994): 8.

New Jewish Agenda. *The Shalom Seders: Three Haggadahs.* New York: Adama Books, 1984.

New Jewish Agenda

---. "AIDS Workgroup Forms." *Gesher* 1:3, October 1986: 3.

---. "Arab-Jewish Dialogue Influences Nairobi Women's Conference." Press Release, July 23 1985.

---. "Call for a 1980 Congress of Progressive Jews," NJA Archive, 1979. Included in this volume, Appendix I. http://newjewisha-genda.wordpress.com/?attachment_id=181

---."Call for a West Bank Settlement Freeze," Newsletter #12, Spring 1983:1 and insert.

---."Chapter Reports." *Gesher* 2:1, October 1987: 5.

---."Conference Survey Results," NJA Newsletter #8, Fall 1981.

---."National Platform," Published Memo, 1982. Included in this volume, Appendix III.

---."Coming Out/Coming Home." Pamphlet, 1985. http://newjewishagenda.files.wordpress.com/2011/11/coming_out_coming_home.pdf

---."Conference For A New Jewish Agenda for the 1980's" Booklet, Washington DC, 1980.

---." Israeli and Palestinian Women in Dialogue, A Search for Peace." Pamphlet, 1985. http://newjewishagenda.wordpress.com/?attachment_id=173

---."Jews and Central America, The Need to Act." Pamphlet. http://newjewishagenda.wordpress.com/?attachment_id=183

---."Jews and the Sanctuary Movement." Pamplet. http://newjewishagenda.wordpress.com/?attachment_id=178

---."NJA Confronts Attacks from the Right." Newsletter #10, Summer 1982: 3.

---."Perspectives on 'Chapter Autonomy'." Newsletter #10, Summer 1982: 3.

---."Preliminary Response to 'New Jewish Agenda: Dissent or Disloyalty?'" http://newjewishagenda.wordpress.com/?attachment_id=189

---."Proposed Minutes, NJA National Steering Committee Meeting." Jan 9-11, 1988.

---."Proposed Mission." 1987. http://newjewishagenda.wordpress.com/?attachment_id=188

---.Some Examples of our Work, 1982. http://newjewishagenda.files.
wordpress.com/2011/11/some1982actions.pdf

---."State of the Organization Report", October 1987.

---."Three Rabbis Excommunicate New Jewish Agenda Members."
NJA Newsletter, Winter 1983: 7. http://newjewishagenda.word-
press.com/?attachment_id=137

"NJA Says 'Fraudulent' Letters Seeking to Disrupt Work of Group."
Jewish Telegraphic Agency. Jul 13, 1982.

"Occupy Judaism." Tumblr. www.blog.occupyjudaism.org/ (accessed
December 12, 2011).

Oppenheim, Carolyn Toll. "The Road To Middle East Peace." *In The
Challenge of Shalom: the Jewish Tradition of Peace and Justice,* edited by
Murray Polner, Naomi Goodman, 119-128. Philadelphia, PA:
New Society Publishers, 1994.

---."The Risks of Silence." OCNJA Newsletter, 1980. http://newjew-
ishagenda.wordpress.com/?attachment_id=187

Orenstein, Debra. "Tisha B'Av – Nagasaki Day." NJA Newsletter #8,
Autumn 1981: 1.

Perlstein, Donny, and Rabbi Gerry Serotta. "Jewish Renewal: The
Birth of an Organization Whose Time Has Come." *Genesis* 2. Sept
– Oct, 1980.

Pogrebin, Letty Cottin. *Deborah, Golda, and Me: Being Female and Jewish in
America.* New York: Crown Publishers, 1991.

Reinheimer, Irit. Personal interview. 3 March 2006.

Reinheimer, Irit and Michael Chameides. *Young, Jewish, and Left.* (2006),
DVD.

Rich, Adrienne. "Reflections on Being a Jewish Progressive in 1985"
Speech to NJA National Convention, 1985. http://www.thesha-
lomcenter.org/content/reflections-being-jewish-progressive-1985

Rogow, Faith. "Why is this Decade Different from all Other Decades?: A Look at the rise of Jewish Lesbian Feminism," *Bridges: A Journal for Jewish Feminists and our Friends* 1:1 (Spring 1990): 67-77.

Rose, Avi. "Co-Chair's Letter." NJA Newsletter, March 1986.

---.Interview by author. Phone interview. January 18, 2006.

---.Letter about Re-Evaluation Counseling in NJA. http://newjewisha-genda.wordpress.com/?attachment_id=180

---."October in Washington." *Gesher* Newsletter 2:2, Jan 1988: 1.

Rosenblit, Avi Daniel. "The New Jewish Agenda and the Lebanon War: Negotiating a discourse in pro-Israel American Jewish identity, 1980-1983" Undergraduate Honors Thesis. Northwestern University, 2003. [in the quote referenced, Rosenblit cites: "Poll: Israel Loses Ground." Newsweek. 4 Oct. 1982.]

Rosenblum, April. "The Past Didn't Go Anywhere: Making Resistance to Antisemitism Part of All of Our Movements." Pintele Yid. Accessed January 25, 2011. http://pinteleyid.com/past-booklet.pdf.

Rudd, Mark. "Mark Rudd — Why Were There So Many Jews in SDS? (or, The Ordeal of Civility)." MarkRudd.com. Accessed Oct 12, 2011. www.markrudd.com/?about-mark-rudd/why-were-there-so-many-jews-in-sds-or-the-ordeal-of-civility.html.

Saidel-Wolk, Rochelle. "New Jewish Group Hopes to Create Progressive-minded National Membership Organization." *Jewish Telegraphic Agency*. Dec 26, 1980.

Schulman, Sarah. *My American History: Lesbian and Gay Life During the Reagan/Bush Years*. New York: Routledge, 1994.

Serotta, Gerry. Interview by author. Personal interview. Silver Springs, MD, July 7 and 11, 2004.

---.Interview by author. Email interview. November 2, 2005.

Silver, Helen. "Special Services Held on the Eve of the March on Washington." *Jewish Telegraphic Agency*. Aug 29, 1983.

Silverstein, Richard. "Earl Krugel: Death of an American Jewish Terrorist." *Tikun Olam*, Last modified Aug 11 1985, access date Jan 25, 2012. http://www.richardsilverstein.com/tikun_olam/2005/11/08/earl-krugel-death-of-an-american-jewish-terrorist/.

Staub, Michael E. "If We Really Care About Israel: Breira and the Limits of Dissent." *In Torn at the Roots the Crisis of Jewish Liberalism in Postwar America*. New York: Columbia University Press, 2002.

Solomonow, Allan. "A New Agenda for American Jews" WIN. Feb 15 1981. http://newjewishagenda.files.wordpress.com/2011/11/new-agenda-for-american-jews.pdf

Thompson, Becky W.. "Central American Peace Movement." *A Promise and a Way of Life: White Antiracist Activism*. Minneapolis: University of Minnesota Press, 2001: 235-265.

Timerman, Jacobo. *Prisoner Without a Name, Cell Without a Number.* New York: Vintage Books, 1982.

Trachtenberg, Bob. "Disarmament," NJA Newsletter #9, Spring 1981: 1.

Waskow, Arthur Ocean. *The Freedom Seder; a New Haggadah for Passover,* 1st ed. New York: Holt, Rinehart, Winston; [mail distribution by] Micah Press, Washington, 1970.

Waskow, Rabbi Arthur. *Seasons of our Joy.* Boston: Beacon Press, 1982.

Wernick, Laura and Leila Wice. "Conference Report: The 12th International Conference of Lesbian and Gay Jews." *Bridges: A Journal for Jewish Feminists and our Friends.* 2:2 (Fall 1991): 129.

Zuckoff, Murray. "At the GA of the CJF: Resolution on the Mideast Emphasizes Importance of U.S.-Israel Being in Accord." *Jewish Telegraphic Agency.* Nov 23, 1983.

Works Cited for **There is an Alternative: Historical Storytelling & Political Practice** by Rachel Mattson:

Berger, Joseph, "Adrienne Cooper, Yiddish Singer, Dies at 65," *New York Times*, December 28, 2011.

Brostoff, Marissa, "Beyond Repair," *Tablet*, September 3, 2010.

Carr, C., "The Bohemian Diaspora," *The Village Voice*, February 4, 1992.

Duncombe, Stephen, *Notes from Underground: Zines and the Politics of Alternative Culture* (Verso, 1997).

Glenn, Susan, *Daughters of the Shtetl: Life and Labor in the Immigrant Generation* (Cornell University Press, 1991).

Green, Adam and Charles Payne, eds., *Time Longer than Rope: A Century of African American Activism, 1850-1950* (NYU Press, 2003).

Howe, Irving, *World of Our Fathers: The Journey of the East European Jews to America and the Life They Found and Made* (Simon and Schuster, 1976).

Irie, Ellen, and Jill Blair (BTW Consultants, Inc.), "Jewish Service Learning: What is and What Could Be: A Summary of an Analysis of the Jewish Service Learning Landscape," commissioned by the Charles and Lynn Schusterman Family Foundation, May 2008.

Jacobs, Jill, "The History of Tikkun Olam," *Zeek*, June 2007.

Keret, Etgar "What of this Goldfish Would You Wish?" in *Suddenly, a Knock on the Door: Stories* (Farrar, Straus and Giroux, 2012).

Kun, Josh, "Bagels, Bongos and Yiddishe Mambos, or The Other History of Jews in America" *Shofar: An Interdisciplinary Journal of Jewish Studies* 23(4) 2005.

Minkin, Sarah Anne, "Daniel Kahn on A Tradition of Subversion and a Subversive Tradition," *Jvoices.com*, March 27, 2009.

North, Michael, "We Have Our Eye on You… So Watch Out, *Times Higher Education*, January 28, 2005.

Rogin, Michael, *Blackface, White Noise: Jewish Immigrants in the Hollywood Melting Pot (University of North Carolina Press, 1998).*

Staub, Michael, *Torn at the Roots: The Crisis of Jewish Liberalism in Postwar America* (Columbia University Press, 2002).